CHRISTIAN PERSPECTIVES ON HUMAN RIGHTS AND LEGAL PHILOSOPHY

Christian Perspectives on Human Rights and Legal Philosophy

Edited by
Paul R. Beaumont

paternoster press

Paternoster Press is an imprint of Paternoster Publishing,
PO Box 300, Carlisle, Cumbria, CA3 0QS, UK
http://www.paternoster-publishing.com

British Library Cataloguing in Publication Data
A catalogue record for this book is available from the British Library

ISBN 0-85364-901-4

This book is printed using Suffolk New Book paper which is 100% acid free

Cover Design by Mainstream, Lancaster
Typeset by WestKey Ltd, Falmouth, Cornwall
Printed in Great Britain by Clays Ltd, Bungay, Suffolk

For David and Anna Beaumont

Contents

Contributors

Paul Beaumont, Professor of European Union and Private International Law, University of Aberdeen

Matthijs de Blois, Lecturer in Law, University of Utrecht

Ian Leigh, Solicitor, Professor of Law, University of Durham

Hilaire McCoubrey, Reverend, Professor of Law and Director of Postgraduate Affairs, University of Hull

John Warwick Montgomery, Barrister, Professor Emeritus of Law and Humanities, University of Luton; Distinguished Professor of Law, Regent University, Virginia, USA; and Senior Counsel, European Centre for Law and Justice

Thomas Glyn Watkin, Reverend, Barrister, Reader in Law, Cardiff Law School, University of Wales

Introduction

Paul Beaumont

This is the second in a series of books on *Christian Perspectives on Law* published by Paternoster Press. The introduction to the first book, *Christian Perspectives on Law Reform* (Beaumont, P.R. (ed.), Carlisle, Paternoster, 1998), explains some of the background to the series. *Christian Perspectives on Law Reform* is an edited collection of expanded versions of some of the papers given at the first Lawyers Christian Fellowship (LCF) Academic Conference at London Bible College on 13 September 1996. This book contains significantly revised and ex‑panded versions of the principal papers given at the second LCF Academic Conference at the University of Bristol on 12 September 1997. It is intended that the third book in the series will be entitled *Christian Perspectives on Law and Relationism* and will flow out of the papers to be presented at the third LCF Academic Conference at the University of Aberdeen on 11 September 1998.

These books constitute a concerted attempt to develop an academically respectable, new legal literature for the new millennium from a Christian worldview. The writers hold, or have held, established academic positions in European universities. The established patterns of academic scrutiny have been applied to the papers. The initial call for papers at each conference has allowed for a process of academic scrutiny and selection. More significantly, the papers from each conference which have been selected for inclusion in the books have been substantially revised by each contributor and again in response to the comments of the editor and the anonymous, independent, academic referees. The books in this series are an unashamed attempt to fill an enormous gap in modern legal writing in Western Europe. There are plenty of books and articles about the law or legal theory written from the predominant liberal, humanist perspec‑tive, whether that viewpoint is explicit or can be inferred; from numerous other theoretical positions like postmodernism and Marxism (now rather unfashionable); and from the standpoint of other religions like Islam. Many modern writers on the law have no doubt been influenced by their Christian beliefs but have seldom explicitly based their arguments on a coherently argued Christian worldview.

The first two books in this series are just the beginning of this task of creating a new corpus of legal materials which can inform Christian lawyers of ways of looking at the law which are consistent with their beliefs and which can take their place in the market-place of ideas with some hope of influencing legal opinion formers. Christians believe that the best and most fulfilling way to live on earth is to follow the good shepherd, the Lord Jesus Christ (Jn. 10:10). It is not the intention of this book and this series simply to reinforce the academic backbone of the existing Christian minority, welcome though that would be, but rather to reach out beyond the fold to the majority of those connected with the law who are not Christians. As Jesus says in John 10:16: 'I have other sheep that are not of this sheep pen. I must bring them also. They too will listen to my voice, and there shall be one flock and one shepherd.'

Most of the essays in these first two books are a first attempt by their authors to examine systematically the substantive issues they are dealing with from a Christian perspective. They are often having to turn over the ground for the first time as well as attempting to plant good seeds. This is not an easy task, and Christians should be grateful for the groundbreaking work accomplished on their behalf. The authors would be the first to acknowledge that much remains to be done to plough parts of the field not yet reached and to bring on the ideas planted in their initial work.

The first two chapters of this book address human rights. Both have interesting things to say about the problem of the public / private divide in the application of human rights. Traditionally human rights have been seen from a public law perspective as rights that individuals can invoke in their relationships with the State. However, the privatisation of human rights is a feature of the Dutch Equal Treatment Act of 1994 considered by Matthijs de Blois and a concern in the debates over the Human Rights Bill in the United Kingdom, especially in the context of the broad definition of a 'public authority', analysed by Ian Leigh. Both authors address the problems which arise in the clash of human rights, particularly between freedom of religion and freedom of speech (Leigh's treatment of blasphemy) and between freedom of religion and equality (non-discrimination) (see de Blois's discussion of the Dutch Equal Treatment Act and Leigh's discourse on the UK Human Rights Bill). The solution offered by de Blois is to make freedom of religion the paramount human right. De Blois is an advocate of human rights from a Christian perspective and therefore his chapter provides a useful balance to that offered by Julian Rivers in the first book of the series in his somewhat sceptical view of the utility of entrenching human rights in UK law (see 'A Bill of Rights for the United Kingdom?' in *Christian Perspectives on Law Reform*, cited above). Leigh's chapter helpfully updates the story told by Rivers of the Labour Government's plans to introduce a Bill of Rights into UK law by analysing the Bill as it stood after its passage through the House of Lords and the completion of the committee stage in the House of Commons.

Matthijs de Blois points out the difficulty of justifying giving rights to humans rather than animals in the absence of a conception that people alone of all creatures on earth are made in God's image. This fact is the basis for the first of his three biblically based principles which he sees as foundational to human rights: dignity, equality and freedom. The second of these principles extends as far as being a basis for some economic rights, in particular the right to social security.

Ian Leigh engages in a prolonged critique of Liberal perspectives on human rights, both from his own external perspective as a Christian and by referring to the works of internal Liberal critics. He helpfully exposes one of the tensions facing Liberals: the problems they have with tolerating those who behave in ways they dislike because of the absolute nature of their religious beliefs. Liberals are in danger of making equality of treatment an absolute and thereby becoming intolerant of those who think there are higher values at stake, e.g. insisting that church schools should employ non-Christians as teachers or forcing such schools into the private sector. Leigh will please Liberals with his critique of the blasphemy laws in England and Wales: God has nothing to fear from free speech. His analysis of the Human Rights Act, however, points up some possible difficulties for orthodox Christian standpoints in the era of the British judiciary applying human rights law.

John Warwick Montgomery gives a stimulating analysis of two of the great schools of legal philosophy and notes what he regards as the downward spiral – from natural law based on biblical revelation, to natural law based on man's reason, to legal positivism where the rules of law in any given legal system do not necessarily reflect high moral standards. Of course legal philosophy also embraces a theory that law is entirely driven by economics as well as a theory that continues the downward spiral beyond legal positivism into the world of deconstructionism where not only are legal rules not required to be moral but those legal rules lack any clear meaning. He appeals for legal theorists to find the basis of law in biblical principles. Of course other perspectives on legal philosophy are consistent with Christian belief. It is possible for a Christian to take a legal positivist position and argue that the law in a particular system is that which is laid down in accordance with that State's Grundnorm or rule of recognition. If the law is incompatible with biblical principles the Christian does not need to claim that it is not law but rather that it is a bad law which should be reformed. On this view biblical principles do not tell us what the law is but rather give us guidance as to what the law should be.

Thomas Watkin goes against the grain of recent experience and argues that security of tenure in employment is good and a sign of God's grace. He illustrates his view by reference to tenants in the time of Henry II, Italian magistrates, Anglican clergy and academics. The paper is a brave and radical attempt to take a biblical concept – *hesed*, translated as steadfastness – and see how it can be applied to contemporary employment. Watkin skilfully addresses some of the expected reactions to such a thesis in a generation brought up on the concept that no one should have a job for life. Even if readers are not entirely convinced by Watkin's arguments they will be stimulated to think again and to question their own presuppositions.

Hilaire McCoubrey tackles one of the most fundamental issues of legal philosophy and human rights – can war ever be justified? He quickly dismisses the concept of a holy war as being in any way justified in the light of New Testament teaching and instead analyses the respective merits of Christian pacifism and a just war. The discourse considers biblical principles and the development of International law. He finds modern International law's prohibition on aggression entirely consistent with a Christian position. McCoubrey recognises the validity of the pacifist approach for a Christian but himself favours the limited use of force currently permitted by International law in terms of collective security against acts of aggression authorised by the United Nations and necessary acts of self-defence by States as permitted by the UN Charter. McCoubrey also outlines the International law applicable to the control of weapons of warfare and to the treatment of prisoners of war and of non-combatants. Once again he finds the current legal standards broadly consistent with a Christian approach.

The contributors and the editor have decided that the royalties from this book will be paid to LCF. The views expressed in the book are personal to the individual contributors who stated them and should not be read as LCF policy. Law students, trainee solicitors, pupils, devils, barristers, advocates, solicitors, judges, para-legals and legal academics are all very welcome to join the LCF and help to increase its capacity to extend the kingdom of God. Further information and application forms can be obtained from Alan and Joyce Holloway, Treasurer and Secretary of the LCF, 20 Waterside Drive, Mearns Park, Newton Mearns, Glasgow G77 6TL (Telephone 0141 616 0522, e-mail LCFadmin@compuserve.com). Readers are welcome to contact the editor of this book on p.beaumont@abdn.ac.uk. The editor acts as the co-ordinator of LCF's academic activities. Readers should note that the LCF is a UK organisation but that similar bodies exist in a number of other countries. Alan and Joyce Holloway have contact details for many of these groupings of Christian lawyers.

I would like to thank Professor David Clarke and Julian Rivers of the University of Bristol for hosting the 1997 LCF Academic Conference and helping to make it a very enjoyable experience for all who partici - pated. The conference was enlivened by the presence of a large group of delegates from the Kenya Christian Lawyers Fellowship and by excellent workshop papers by Richard Townshend-Smith, Christa Tobler, Robert West, Alan Robinson and Nazila Ghanea-Hercock. Much of the burden of dealing with the bookings for the conference was handled by my colleague at the University of Aberdeen, Keith Wotherspoon, and for this and many other examples of efficient administration I am very grateful. Important and much-appreciated practical assistance at the conference was provided by James Wakefield (LCF Student and Young Lawyer Co-ordinator) and Chris Pain (LCF General Assistant).

In relation to the preparation of the book I wish to record my thanks to each of the contributors for their hard work and forbearance with deadlines and requests for revisals. Each contribution was scrutinised by the editor and at least one anonymous referee. Very sincere thanks are offered to those who gave of their time as referees knowing that they would gain no financial reward or public recognition. [1] Once again I am pleased to be able to thank Maureen Mercer and Amanda Walton, secretaries in the Department of Law at the University of Aberdeen, for their invaluable assistance in preparations for the conference and in helping prepare the manuscript for the publisher. Finally, it is good to have the opportunity to thank all those at Paternoster Publishing who have been involved in any way in the commissioning, production and promotion of the books in this series.

This book is dedicated to my two children, David, seven, and Anna, six. Every parent wants their children to have happy and fulfilled lives. I know that if they model their lives on their grandmother, to whom the first book in the series was dedicated, they will grow up to love the Lord Jesus Christ and be effective witnesses to God's capacity to fill our lives with peace, meaning and hope. David and Anna fill my life with love and affection. It is an enormous privilege being a father and receiving such faith and trust. Good parent–child relationships are foundational to society, as I am sure we will begin to explore in the third book in the series. Finally, let me conclude this paragraph of personal indulgence by thanking my wife Marion for working very hard as a chartered accountant and at parenting, sharing my faith and loving me.

Good Friday 1998

---

[1] Special thanks are due to Caroline Robertson, a recent University of Aberdeen law graduate, who prepared the index.

The Foundation of Human Rights
A Christian Perspective

Matthijs de Blois

I. Introduction

Imagine you are working as an official of the UN in former Yugoslavia. You are staying in an isolated, besieged little town. There are no communications with the outside world. You are responsible for the distribution of food. There is only one bag of flour left. There are two institutions which are candidates for the flour, both desperately in need of food. In the first place a home for elderly, demented people and secondly a small zoo where they have a group of a rare breed of chimpanzees, threatened by extinction. Both need the complete bag to let their inmates survive. It is not possible to split up the bag of flour, unless at least some elderly people and some chimps die. What is your choice?

Over a number of years I have confronted students with this question in my seminar on the Philosophy of Human Rights, which is part of our special programme for foreign students. It is striking that the response is very diverse. I have had groups in which almost 100 per cent opted for the elderly, but also groups where half of the students opted for the chimps. I was of course primarily interested in their arguments. Making a choice is one thing, explaining why one chooses for either the elderly people or the chimps another. Most of the students did not come further than emotive arguments, such as 'I have a nice grand-mother, therefore I opt for the elderly', 'because I am a human being my choice is for the human beings' and 'there are so many human beings compared to this rare breed of chimps, I prefer to give the food to the latter'.

These answers do not surprise me since the general climate in these postmodern days is one of the rejection of the possibility of formulating a foundation for whatever moral point of view is adopted. So 'founda-tionalism' is out-dated. The popular American philosopher Richard Rorty made this clear in his Oxford Amnesty lecture on human rights in 1993. He claims that 'nothing relevant to moral choice separates human beings from animals except historically contingent facts of the world, cultural facts'.[1] We have according to Rorty no knowledge of the special nature of human beings, which serves as a foundation of the respect for human dignity. As an explanation for this he points at Darwinism, which deprived most intellectuals of the idea that there is something special about human beings compared to animals (Darwinists tend to say 'other animals'). Nevertheless Rorty's objective remains to bring about the utopia sketched by the Enlightenment – including the protection of human rights. But how is this to be achieved if it is not possible to refer to a decisive moral argument which makes clear that we are morally bound to protect human rights? Rorty's answer is: by manipulation of sentiments. His expectation is that bringing sad stories on television about violations of human rights in all parts of the world will motivate people to do something about it, just as the publication of Harriet Beecher Stowes' *Uncle Tom's Cabin* did bring about sympathy for the American slaves. I am not at all convinced that things work like that. I doubt whether frequent confrontation on television with the suffering of others does by definition result in sympathy and a general conviction that the violation of human rights is morally wrong. It may on the contrary lead to indifference towards the suffering of fellow human beings. As long as it is far away in some foreign country. . . .

Even if it would work like that, who will guarantee that the same device is not used to incite people to racial or religious hatred, as the Nazis used to do and media in some Arab countries still do? Furthermore, why should we bring about the utopia sketched by the Enlightenment – why not the communist utopia, the *Third Reich* or a Muslim state?

In order to defend the case of human rights we need more than sentiments or emotions. We need a solid rock to stand on. As a Christian I am convinced that there is such a rock: the only foundation, which is our Lord Jesus Christ (1 Cor. 3:11). He is decisive for all aspects of our lives, including the field of morality.[2]

II. Christian Morality: The Morality of Christians[3]

Terminological clarification

Morality and *ethics* are used here as exchangeable concepts. They are used in a normative sense.

1   R. Rorty, 'Human Rights: Rationality and Sentimentality', in S. Shute and S. Hurley (eds.), *On Human Rights*, (New York, 1993), 112–134, at 116.
2   Of course Rorty will not be convinced by this point of view. He will consider Christianity just as another historically contingent cultural fact.
3   Compare B. Kay and G. Wenham (eds.), *Law, Morality and the Bible*, (Leicester, 1978).

Morality, or ethics, refers to standards (values, principles, norms) for human behaviour. Standards may have different degrees of abstraction, which cannot always be sharply distinguished. Morality, or ethics, con - cerns motives as well as actions in both our personal life and in our life as members of social groups: the family, the church, the State. It has to be underlined in this connection that the personal and the social are closely connected, as we are created as individuals indeed, but to a great extent are dependent on other people and institutions.

A Christian is a person who belongs to Jesus Christ, a person who believes in Jesus as his or her Lord and Saviour and has received the Holy Spirit. 'If anyone is in Christ, he is a new creation' (2 Cor. 5:17). Being a new creation implies that we are no longer slaves of sin, having become slaves of righteousness to serve God, as we learn from Romans 6, which is one of the key passages in the New Testament on ethics. Morality is in essence serving the Lord, it is part of our sanctification. Being born again implies that both knowledge of the will of God (Rom. 12:2) and a life in accordance with it becomes possible. Living the new life results from renewal into the likeness of Christ (2 Cor. 3:15–4:6), it is the fruit of the Spirit (Gal. 5:22).

True knowledge of God's will depends on revelation, that is the Bible as the Word of God, and the guidance of the Holy Spirit. In the Bible we do not find a sharp distinction between doctrine as such and morality, or between theology and ethics. The teachings of the Bible on God's character and his plan for mankind, the person and work of Jesus Christ, the nature and destiny of man, the work of the Holy Spirit, and many more aspects of Christian doctrine are relevant for morality. Christian morality is essentially a response to God's love for human beings: '. . . be merciful, just as your Father is merciful' (Lk. 6:36).

The Christian presence in the world

In order to see what Christian morality requires in the field of human rights, that is, in the field of the law, it is important to realise first of all what our position is as Christians in this world. The New Testament does not provide us with a blueprint of the perfect legal order or of the 'Christian' state, including perhaps a Bill of Rights. That is not by chance.

In the Old Testament we see that the people of God, Israel, is elected to be a nation living in a specific geographic area, the promised land, in a community in which the religious, political and legal cannot be separated. In modern terms: church and state were intertwined. It was a theocracy, based on the *Torah*.

From the New Testament it becomes clear that the birth of the church marks a new phase in the history of God with mankind. There is continuity, but also discontinuity, between the Old and the New Testaments. The position of Christians differs in many respects from that of the Israelites. The church is not a national entity. It consists of people from all nations, tribes, peoples and tongues, united by their common belief in the Lord Jesus Christ, who is the head of the church. We are *in* this world, but no longer *of* this world (Jn. 17). We are, just as our Lord, outside the camp of this world, seeking the city to come (Heb. 13:12–14). The kingdom of God still has a hidden character. It waits to be established in all its power and glory by the King in the future (Rev. 20:1–6). This has important consequences for the possible role of Christian morality in this world. It makes clear that it is not up to Christians to build the kingdom of God, including its moral component, by means of outward physical force, as has been tried in the past more than once. We only have to think of the disastrous effort to establish a so-called Kingdom of the New Zion in the first part of the sixteenth century. [4] The Bible shows us another way.

Morality as part of our witness

As Christians we are called in this present world to be witnesses of the Lord in words and deeds. We are the salt of the earth and as such a preserving force against corruption (Mt. 5:12). We are the light of the world, called to shine before men, that they may see our good works and glorify our Father in heaven (Mt. 5:14–16). These texts refer in the first place to our own behaviour. An exemplary way of life is required of disciples. Next to that, however, it is part of our witness to exert a positive influence on the behaviour of other people for their well-being and, to the extent we are in a position to influence it, by the formulation and the application of the law. In this we should be guided by the moral principles revealed in the Bible, taking into account what has been said about our position and what will be said on the pluralistic character of society.

The pluralistic society

The world, the society, in which we live is essentially pluralistic in character. That means that members of society have different and often incompatible opinions in respect of both the foundation and the contents of morality. These divisions include the diverging answers to the question of the role of the State and the law to enforce moral principles in society. This pluralism is in my view not a recent development. We could even say that pluralism is a consequence of the existence of the church as an 'alien' entity in this world. Therefore it cannot be simply said that all

---

[4]   I am referring to an attempt by some 'anabaptists' to establish this kingdom by violent means. This movement was strongly opposed by the Reformer Menno Simons. Compare E.H. Broadbent, *The Pilgrim Church*, (1931), (Southampton, 1989), 179–185.

human beings should conform to Christian ethical principles. Of course, the gospel should be preached to all human beings, to the whole of creation (Mt. 28:19; Mk. 16:15). The call to conversion is universal. Living in accordance with the will of God is the only truly fulfilled way to live (Jn. 10:10). All human beings are responsible to their creator for the way they comply with God's commandments (Rom. 1:18–32). This being said on the moral responsibility of all human beings, it is at the same time clear from the New Testament that of the disciples of Christ a more excellent life is required than the life to be expected from other human beings. The command to turn one's other cheek can be required of a Christian but is not meant to abolish the exception of self-defence in criminal law. There is an inside and an outside. We are called to judge those belonging to the church, but God judges those who are outside (1 Cor. 5:13). The freedom we claim for ourselves we cannot deny other people: 'do to others what you would have them do to you, for this sums up the Law and the Prophets' (Mt. 7:12).

It is essential that we try to ensure that in our society people will have the possibility of finding their temporal and eternal destiny, that is, that they come to a living relationship with their creator, which also leads to the best possible relationship with their fellow human beings.

III. Law and Morality

Dealing rather extensively with morality in a chapter on human rights suggests already that morality has something to do with the law. Indeed it has.[5] It is tempting to dwell here on the classical discussion between Naturalism and Legal Positivism.[6] I will restrict myself to the remark that my approach is similar to the Naturalist one by underlining a relationship between law and morality in the sense that morality – here understood as Christian morality – functions as a critical standard for the evaluation of the law. I do not agree, however, with the claim of Naturalism that moral principles can be derived in a purely rational way. I have referred to the revelation and the guidance of the Holy Spirit as necessary for the understanding of God's will also in the field of morality. This does not exclude of course the use of reason 'within the bounds of revelation'.[7] Reason is a gift of God, also to be used to decide what is right and wrong with regard to the biblical principles.

[5] Compare also Norman Anderson, *Freedom under Law*, (Eastbourne, 1988), 79–103.

[6] Compare John Finnis, *Natural Law and Natural Rights*, (Oxford, 1980) and H.L.A. Hart, *The Concept of Law*, (Oxford, 1961). See also J.W. Montgomery, 'Why a Christian Philosophy of Law?', chapter 3, below.

[7] With a wink to Nicolas Wolterstorff, *Reason within the Bounds of Religion*, (Grand Rapids, 1984).

This approach cannot be suspected of a kind of naturalistic fallacy. Ought is not derived from Is, but from the Word of God. On the other hand I realise that it will not convince those who like Kelsen want to purify the law from all theology.[8]

Morality should function as a critical standard for the evaluation of the law as it stands. Morality has relevance for the interpretation of the law and for law reform. We are all aware of the fact that law requires interpretation. Working in the field of the law means, in most cases, interpretation of rules. By necessity this brings in morality. The meaning of a rule of law in a specific situation is not always clear. Judges and other decision makers will need concepts – legal principles – as means to interpret the law. These legal principles, it is submitted, have a moral character.

Furthermore, lawyers are involved in the formulation of legal rules, for example in the drafting of legislation. It will be clear that in this field morality will play a role, of course in the framework of a political context. It is common knowledge that rules (e.g. legislation) are made and abolished on moral considerations. Changes in moral ideas will in many cases result in changes to the law.

This does not mean, however, that the concepts of law and morality are synonymous. The role of the law is restricted to ensure peace and justice in public society as a whole. As such the law is a very important prerequisite for the development of individuals and communities in accordance with their destiny. Morality is however also concerned with personal behaviour outside public life. As we will see this is not only a matter of fact, but also a moral principle: the realm of the law should be restricted in order to leave room for human beings to live in accordance with their own moral opinions.

Law will be primarily concerned with the outward behaviour of human beings, irrespective of their inner motives (though in some areas of the law, such as criminal law, motives may play a role). On the other hand, in morality motives play an important role, as does the resulting behaviour.

We will concentrate in the rest of the chapter on the evaluation of human rights – that is, on an important part of the law – from the perspective of Christian morality.

IV. The Foundation of Human Rights

We are all familiar with the notion of human rights in international legal instruments which have entered into force since World War II. Almost without exception they refer to the Universal Declaration of Human

---

[8] Compare Hans Kelsen, *Reine Rechtslehre*, (Vienna, 1960).

Rights, which was adopted on 10 December 1948 by the General Assembly of the United Nations as their source of inspiration.[9] The catalogue of rights embodied therein is still representative of what constitutes human rights. Its first article holds that all human beings are born *free* and *equal dignity* and rights. This is elaborated in articles which provide for freedom of both the body and the mind. Other provisions guarantee equality, not only in a formal but also to a certain extent in a material, sense. They all presuppose the dignity of the human being. While it appeared to be impossible in 1948 to introduce in the text the notion that these rights were God-given,[10] there is a general idea that Christians are in favour of these rights. The suggestion that human rights are *inter alia* inspired by Christianity is at least there. That is illustrated by the speech at the formal inauguration of the European Court of Human Rights at Strasbourg on 20 April 1959 by its first president, Lord McNair. He stated that the words of Jesus Christ in Matthew 25:40 'inasmuch as ye have done it unto one of the least of these my brethren, ye have done it unto me' inspired instruments such as the Universal Declaration of Human Rights.[11]

I should like to stress that human rights are not exclusively inspired by Christianity. On the contrary, they are and have been defended by representatives of other worldviews, philosophies and religions. We have seen recently that within Islam human rights are formulated and defended.[12]

Next to that, we see in the western world that for adherents of liberal political philosophy human rights are the core of their theory.[13] In history their predecessors, the philosophers of the Enlightenment, strongly promoted the enactment of human rights in constitutional documents.[14] We will see below, however, that long before the eighteenth-century Enlightenment a connection between Christianity and principles on the protection of human beings, similar to those which are now codified as

[9] Compare, e.g., the Preambles to the European Convention for the Protection of Human Rights and Fundamental Freedoms (Rome, 1950) and the International Covenant on Civil and Political Rights (New York, 1966).

[10] Compare Johannes Morsink, 'The Philosophy of the Universal Declaration', 6 *Human Rights Quarterly* (1984), 309–334, at 312–314.

[11] *Yearbook of the European Convention on Human Rights 1958–1959*, (The Hague, 1960), 154.

[12] Compare the Arab Charter on Human Rights, *The Review* No. 56 / 1996, 57, (International Commission of Jurists) and, e.g., A.K. Brohi, 'The Nature of Islamic Law and the Concept of Human Rights', in *Human Rights in Islam*, (Geneva, 1982), 43–60.

[13] Compare, e.g., John Rawls, *A Theory of Justice*, (Oxford, 1973). See Ian Leigh, 'Towards a Christian Approach to Religious Liberty', chapter 2 below.

[14] Compare J.M. Kelly, *A Short History of Western Legal Theory*, (Oxford, 1993), 268–271.

human rights, can be discerned. That will become clear when we discuss the role of the Reformation with respect to religious freedom.

Our argument is, nevertheless, not primarily historical. We will investigate whether the three basic and interrelated values which can be seen as the core of human rights: *dignity*, *equality* and *freedom*, can be founded in Christian morality.

Dignity

For a Christian view of the foundation of human rights we start with God as the creator of all things. He called the world and everything in it into being to his glory. He created man as the crown of his creation:

> Then God said, 'Let us make man in Our image, in Our likeness; and let them rule over the fish of the sea, and the birds of the air, and over the livestock, and over all the earth, and over all the creatures that move along the ground.' So God created man in his own image, in the image of God he created him; male and female he created them. (Gen. 1:26–27)

This reveals to us fundamental truths concerning every human being, every human being. First of all we see his (and her) *special position* in the creation. The text from Genesis provides us with the decisive argument against the rather popular idea that a human being is just an intelligent kind of primate and that there is no reason for the special treatment of human beings compared to other creatures. It is the answer to the Darwinism referred to by Rorty. With reason therefore we can maintain that human rights deserve special attention.

Furthermore, the fact that man is created by God makes clear that his or her existence is dependent on God's will; in biblical perspective all human beings are 'wanted'. It is clear from the Bible that the creation of man is realised by formation in the womb: 'you knit me together in my mother's womb' (Ps. 139:13).

The special position of human beings because of their creation in God's image extends to the unborn as well. Similarly also the deformed and handicapped are created by the Lord (Ex. 4:11) in his image.

The creation of man in God's image and likeness has important moral implications.[15] First of all it makes clear why we have to recognise the dignity of each and every individual human being as such. All human beings are worthy of respect, irrespective of any additional quality such

---

[15] Compare the excellent study by Gary B. Ferngern, 'The *Imago Dei* and the Sanctity of Life: The Origins of an Idea', in Richard C. McMillan, H. Tristram Engelhardt Jr. and Stuart Spicker, (eds.), *Euthanasia and the Newborn*, (Dordrecht, Lancaster, Reidel, 1987), 23–45. See also J.I. Packer, 'Conscience, Choice and Character' in B. Kay and G. Wenham (eds.), *Law, Morality and the Bible*, (Leicester, 1978), 168–192.

as nationality, intelligence, age or social status. It is clear from both the Old and the New Testaments that the notion of being created in God's image and likeness has consequences for our behaviour towards other human beings. Both the life and the honour of human beings should be protected (Gen. 9:6 and Jas. 3:9). The creation in the image and likeness of God implies also that man is created with a purpose. He or she is a responsible person, called to live in communication with his or her creator, to respond to God's demands, to reflect his glory. Human beings are called to preserve and develop the earth. Mankind is therefore created with freedom to choose, to make decisions, to choose a path of life, in short he is a moral being we have to respect as such.

The first pages of the Bible make clear that people are not created only as individuals to live on their own. The verse quoted stresses 'male and female he created them'. That means that people are created to live in communion with other people. Not only the individual, but also the communities of individuals, such as marriage and families, deserve respect.

Genesis 3 confronts us with the disastrous result of Adam and Eve's use of their freedom: the Fall, which brought sin into the world. This should not be overlooked in the discussion of the theme of human rights. It explains the violation of the dignity and worth of so many human beings in this world by the sinful acts of others. It also underlines the necessity of governments restricting the freedom of individuals in order to protect others. Finally it may be asked whether the Fall did not result in the loss of the dignity derived from being created in the image and likeness of God? The sinfulness of human beings makes them unworthy in the light of the holiness of God.

However, the best news ever, which is revealed in the Bible from Genesis 3 to Revelation, makes clear that this is not the final word. Mercy triumphs over judgement (Jas. 2:13). The whole Bible is testimony of 'the kindness and love of God our Saviour toward man' (Tit. 3:4). The eternal Son of God, Jesus Christ, became man, to bear the sins of the world on the cross. He died and rose again to save for eternity all who believe in him. If sinful human beings, that means all human beings, are loved by God to this extent, it can only mean that human beings should be loved and respected in human relations. Christians, who know that they have been saved themselves, will be motivated by the doctrine of redemption to defend and pursue the protection of the invaluable worth and dignity of human beings.[16]

What has been said on the creation of people and the offer of redemption for all of us is a reason for supporting the recognition of

---

[16] Compare also P.H. Kooijmans, 'Protestantism and the Development of International Law', *Receuil des Cours de l'Academie de Droit International de la Haye* (1977), Vol. 3, 87–117, at 92.

human rights in law.[17] They provide for the conditions under which the respect for the dignity of human beings in society can be realised. It is therefore not surprising that Christian morality was at least one of the sources of Article 1, Paragraph 1 of the Constitution of the Federal Republic of Germany, which holds that 'The dignity of man shall be inviolable.'[18] From human dignity more specific human rights can be derived, as they translate into legal guarantees of the respect for the human person as such. That does not mean, however, that the whole body of national and international human rights law has automatically received Christian approval. The formulation as well as the interpretation of single human rights should be subjected to a critical appraisal in the light of the biblical basis of human dignity.

A few examples will illustrate this. Contrary to approaches which seem to reserve respect for human dignity only to certain categories of human beings,[19] the biblical approach leads to the recognition of the dignity of all persons whatever their state of development or physical or mental health. The importance of this idea for the interpretation of the right to life and the right to personal integrity in connection with questions such as abortion, experiments on unborn children and the killing of severely handicapped babies will be clear.

This is exemplified by one of the dissenting opinions attached to the Resolution of the Inter-American Commission of Human Rights of

---

[17] Compare among others John Warwick Montgomery, *Human Rights and Human Dignity*, (Edmonton, 1995), especially 189–218; J. Douma, *Ethiek en Recht*, (Kampen, 1990), 46–49; Wolfgang Huber and Heinz Eduard Tödt, *Menschenrechte*, (Berlin, 1978), 181–193; James I. Packer, 'Conscience, Choice and Character', *op. cit.*, n. 15.

[18] Compare Johannes Messner, 'Die Idee der Menschenwürde im Rechtsstaat der pluralistischen Gesellschaft', in Gerhard Leibholz et al (eds.), *Menschen-würde und freiheitliche Rechtsordnung*, (Festschrift Geiger, 1974), 221–241; Klaus Stern, 'Menschenwürde als Wurzel der Menschen- und Grundrechte', in Norbert Achterberg, Werner Krawietz und Dieter Wyduchel (eds.), *Recht und Staat im Sozialen Wandel*, Festschrift für Hans Ulrich Scupin zum 80 (Geburtstag, Berlin, 1983), 627–642.

[19] Compare Kurt Baier, 'When Does the Right to Life Begin?', in, J. Roland Pennock and John W. Chapman (eds.), *Human Rights*, (New York and London, 1981), 201–229. Characteristic of Baier's view is the following quotation: 'I have therefore assumed that normal adults have a natural right to life. . . . when we talk about the right to life of those human beings who are unable to keep alive without assistance, who need life support, we are going beyond the natural right to life. I have argued that where such life support is concerned, we need to draw up classes of need and priorities among these classes and that fetuses are near or at the bottom of the hierarchy of such classes' (224). See for another example of this approach Helga Kuhse and Peter Singer, 'Individuals, Humans and Persons: The Issue of moral status' in Peter Singer (ed.), *Embryo experimentation*, (Cambridge, 1990), 65–75.

6 March 1981 in the so-called *Baby-Boy* case.[20] Central to this case was the question of compatibility of the 'legalisation' of abortion by the American Supreme Court with the recognition of Article 1 of the American Declaration of the Rights and Duties of Man, which holds that 'Every human being has the right to life'. The question was whether this provision excluded abortion. The majority of the Commission said that it did not. Two members of the Commission, however, dissented. One of them, Dr Monroy Cabra, explained why he had come to a different interpretation by referring in his opinion explicitly to the biblical view of human life, by saying that: 'The maternal womb in which the flame of life is lighted is sacred and may not be profaned to extinguish what God has created in his image and likeness.'[21]

He concluded that the relevant provision of the American Declaration indeed implied the protection of unborn human beings from the moment of conception. Next to this the interpretation of human rights in the light of human dignity in a biblical sense makes clear that human beings are created with a purpose. They are here to develop the earth and to find their eternal destiny in a relationship with God through Jesus Christ. Respect for human rights therefore cannot imply that humans should have the right to destroy themselves. This was very aptly formulated by John Locke (1632–1704), who is honoured as the champion of the 'liberal' view of human rights. In describing in his *Second Treatise of Government* the characteristics of the *state of nature*, he writes the following on both the respect for others' as for one's own life:

> though man in that state have an uncontrollable liberty to dispose of his person or possessions, yet he has not liberty to destroy himself . . . no one ought to harm another in his life, health, liberty or possessions; for men being all the workmanship of one omnipotent and infinitely wise Maker; all the servants of one sovereign Master, sent into this world by His order and about His business; they are His property, whose workmanship they are made to last during His, not one another's pleasure. . . . Everyone as he is bound to preserve himself, and not to quit his station wilfully, so by the like reason, . . . ought he as much as he can to preserve the rest of mankind. . . .'[22]

That this approach has important consequences for the interpretation of, for example, the right to privacy, can be illustrated by a recent decision

---

[20]　Resolution No. 23/81 in Case 2141 (United States), *Human Rights Law Journal* 2 (1981), 110–130.

[21]　*Ibid.*, 123.

[22]　John Locke, *Two Treatises of Government*, Book II, chapter II, 6 in Everyman's Library, (Introd. W.S. Carpenter), (London, 1978), 119–120. For a recent analysis of suicide and assisted suicide see J.W. Montgomery, 'Whose Life Anyway? A Re-examination of Suicide and Assisted Suicide', in P. Beaumont (ed.), *Christian Perspectives on Law Reform*, (Carlisle, 1998), 83–103.

of the European Court of Human Rights.[23] Some British nationals were complaining about the fact that they had been prosecuted and sentenced for maltreatment because of their participation in sadistic sexual activities. Their defence was the consent of the victims, which, if individual self-determination was the basic value behind human rights, would indeed have been decisive. The European Court, however, rejected their claim that the United Kingdom had violated Article 8 of the European Convention on Human Rights, the right to privacy. This right was involved, but the punishment of the cruelty could be justified under the restriction clause for the protection of health. In other words, for the European Court the principle of self-determination is not the final word. There appears to be room for an approach which founds human rights in the respect for human dignity in a biblical sense.

Finally, I mention the question of euthanasia, which is often also defended by a reference to self-determination,[24] in connection with the interpretation of the right to life. Christians believe life to be God's gift, as well as something we hold on trust. As was said in a recent study of the Church of Scotland: 'Ultimate authority in matters of life and death rests solely with God from whom that life derives.'[25] Therefore no one has the right to take their own life or to wilfully let their life be taken by another person.[26]

Equality

The creation of people in the image and likeness of God is also the argument for the equal worth and dignity of all human beings. This idea cannot be based on perception. We only perceive that people are equal

[23]   European Court of Human Rights, 19 February 1997, *Laskey, Jaggard and Brown* v *The United Kingdom*, (1997), 24 E.H.R.R. (European Human Rights Reports), 39 (July 1997, Part I). The decision of the House of Lords in this case dates from 11 March 1993 and is known as the case of *R.* v *Brown*, [1993] 2 All ER 75.

[24]   Compare Joanna K. Weinberg, 'Demystifying the Right to Die: The New Jersey Experience', *Medicine and Law*, (1988), 7:323–345; H.J.J. Leenen, 'Dying with Dignity: Developments in the Field of Euthanasia in the Netherlands', *Medicine and Law*, (1989), 8:517–526.

[25]   *Euthanasia: A Christian perspective*, Published on behalf of the Board of Social Responsibility of the Church of Scotland, Edinburgh, 1995, at 14.

[26]   Compare Robert E. Willis, *The Ethics of Karl Barth*, (Leiden, 1971), 376; J. Douma, *Euthanasie*, (Groningen, 1979); Erik Wolf, *Recht des Nächsten. Ein rechtstheologischer Entwurf*, (Frankfurt am Main, 1957), 25; Wilhelm Uhlenbruck, 'Recht auf den eigenen Tod', *Zeitschrift für Rechtspolitik* Heft 9, (September 1986), 209–217 at 212; David Stone, Euthanasia, Fulcrum: *The Journal of the Lawyers Christian Fellowship*, (1991), No. 31, 26–29; and J.W. Montgomery, *op. cit.*, n. 22.

in some respects and unequal in others. From experience we cannot derive essential human equality. The equality between human beings as far as their dignity and worth is concerned can, however, be derived from the Bible.[27] In a recent article Louis Pojman concludes that secular egalitarian arguments for equal rights have not offered plausible reasons for the equal worth of human beings. In his view this doctrine can only be based on the Judeo-Christian tradition.[28]

The Bible stresses the fact that mankind 'was made from one blood' (Acts 17:26). We have one Father, because one God created us (Mal. 2:10). There is also equality in sinfulness between human beings, 'all have sinned and fall short of the glory of God' (Rom. 3:23), but again the offer of salvation is for all. It is God's desire that all people be saved (1 Tim. 2:4). Therefore we find in the church the fundamental rule 'neither Jew nor Greek . . . neither male nor female; for you are all one in Christ Jesus' (Gal. 3:28). James rebukes partiality in the church (Jas. 2).

While society in Paul's and James' days in accordance with classical philosophy and Roman law knew slavery, it was recommended to the Christian master to accept his converted slave as a brother in the Lord (Philem.). Furthermore 'slavetraders' are listed with other examples of lawless people in 1 Timothy 1:10.[29] It has to be said, however, that a revolutionary change was not preached (compare Col. 3:22).

This cannot but influence the behaviour of Christians in society as well. It is not surprising that the efforts to abolish slavery were initiated by Christians such as William Wilberforce.[30] What is surprising, however, is that it took so long to urge for changes in this field.[31]

The question of the equal worth of all human beings is still a topical issue, having regard to the growing number of manifestations of racism,

---

[27] Compare Emil Brunner, *Gerechtigkeit*, (Zürich, 1943), 36–43.

[28] Louis Pojman, 'On Equal Human Worth: A Critique of Contemporary Egalitarianism', in Louis Pojman and Robert Westmoreland (eds.), *Equality: Selected Readings*, (New York, Oxford, 1997), 282–296.

[29] The term is used in the New International Version. Compare also Norman Anderson, *Freedom under Law*, *op. cit.*, n. 5 at 12.

[30] Compare T. Sutton, 'Christians as Law Reformers in the Nineteenth and Twentieth Centuries', in P. Beaumont (ed.), *Christian Perspectives on Law Reform*, (Carlisle, 1998).

[31] I am not completely convinced by the explanations given by Anderson for the fact that it took so long before Christians became aware that slavery was contrary to Christian principles. He mentions three factors: universal usage, economic and social pressure, and the permission of slavery in the Old Testament and the lack of an explicit prohibition in the New Testament; compare his *Freedom under Law*, *op. cit.*, n. 5 at 12. This does not explain why the radical change did not take place before the end of the eighteenth century.

also in the Western world. Racial discrimination, which stems from a non-biblical idea of superiority of certain human beings above others, should be unconditionally condemned. An official policy of racism such as had been legal in South Africa and earlier in the United States should be opposed. It is of great value that Christians such as Martin Luther King have taken a lead in the non-violent resistance against racism.

The equal worth of all human beings in a biblical sense does not mean that all differences in treatment of human beings are excluded. On the contrary, the Bible makes clear that the positions of parents and children, of husband and wife, of Christians and non-Christians may be different. Distinctions between human beings may be part of God's created order. They may also lead to a certain extent to different treatment in a moral and legal sense, corresponding with the different responsibilities con - cerned. Nevertheless, they do not conflict with the fundamental concept of the equal worth of all human beings.

Furthermore, it is clear that the conduct of persons may lead to different treatment. In church as well as in society there can be sanctions for misbehaviour resulting in difference in treatment of human beings. These examples of unequal treatment are never the result of despising certain categories of human beings. Condemnation of sin should be accompanied by love and respect for the sinner (Jn. 8:1–11).

Equality does not mean uniformity or indifference as to (im)moral beliefs or practices. Of course this is recognised not only by Christians. In fact a great part of the law of any country consists of making distinctions between human beings on account of their capabilities (who may enter university), age (voting rights only for adults), behaviour (only criminals should be punished), nationality (only EU-nationals have certain rights under EC-law), etc. Important moral and legal problems may arise from different evaluations as to which distinctions are justified. Again it will be important from which perspective the concept of the equal worth of human beings is interpreted.

This is a topical issue in the Netherlands where we have a so-called General Act on Equal Treatment which entered into force in 1994, after a long and heated discussion on both the need for such an Act and on its precise content. The Act prohibits discrimination – *inter alia* – on the basis of heterosexual or homosexual orientation or civil status. It concerns not only the relationship between government and citizens – which is the classical sphere of application of human rights – but also the relation - ship between citizens among themselves and between citizens and private organisations. It prescribes in other words what we call the 'horizontal' effect of human rights. This introduces a serious problem. There are private organisations in the Netherlands, such as schools, which are founded on biblical principles and which ask from their teachers and students compliance with these principles as far as their private sexual life is concerned. They can invoke the freedom of religion and the freedom to provide education in accordance with one's conviction to support their claim. This is an example of a collision of human rights, which is the logical consequence of the acceptance of the horizontal effect of human rights and which is likely in a society characterised by deep controversies in the field of basic moral values. The Act contains provisions which provide for some exceptions to the rule of equal treatment. They are, however, of an ambiguous nature and it is not at all sure that Christian organisations will remain free to pursue within their own structures the principles in the field of sexual morality they adhere to. There is a tension between equality as interpreted by the legislator and the principle of freedom, which we will discuss below.

The equal worth and dignity of human beings should not only lead to a recognition of formal equality, resulting in an equal legal position between human beings unless there are good reasons for a differential treatment. The equal worth of human beings should also find its expression in a measure of equality in respect of the material means people need for their subsistence and development. It is remarkable that in two of the three places in the Bible where the word 'equality' is used it refers to equality in, at least partly, a material sense. When Paul exhorts the Corinthians to help the church at Jerusalem he refers to the spiritual blessings they had received from Jerusalem, which should motivate them to support this church in its poverty:

> Our desire is not that others might be relieved while you are hard pressed, but that there might be equality. At the present time your plenty will supply what they need, so that in turn their plenty will supply what you need. Then there will be equality, as it is written: 'He that gathered much did not have too much and he that gathered little did not have too little' (2 Cor. 8:13–15).

There are good reasons to defend, on the basis of the equal worth of human beings, social human rights, which are formulated to ensure a just social order in which there are real possibilities for development for all human beings. Concern for the poor and just social relations are fundamental in the Bible.[32] Care for orphans and widows is part of a pure and undefiled religion before God the Father (Jas. 1:27). On the other hand abuses of the rich are criticised, both in the Old and in the New Testaments (Isa. 3:14, Jas. 5:1–5). Private property is not condemned, it is on the contrary to be respected. Its use should, however, not be detrimental to others. This does not provide us with a detailed description of legislation in the social and economic field. It offers, however, sufficient arguments in favour of legal guarantees for social security for those in social and economic need, which is expressed for example in Article 9 of the International Covenant on Economic, Social and Cultural Rights.

---

[32] Compare Ronald J. Sider, *Completely Pro-Life*, (Downers Grove, Illinois, 1987), 73–81; *idem. Rich Christians in an Age of Hunger*, (Downers Grove, Illinois, 1984).

Freedom

A human being is created as a responsible creature. He or she is called to respond to the creator and to develop a living and joyful relationship with God and his or her fellow human beings. We read in Genesis that the first man and woman received a divine command and that they are held responsible for disobedience (Gen. 2, 3). After the Fall man did not lose the possibility of entering into a relationship with God and his or her neighbour. Human beings have not lost their responsibility to develop the earth and to follow the commandments of God. By the offer of grace through Jesus Christ a new relationship with God is possible. The gospel is therefore to be preached to the ends of the earth so that men and women can come to find their eternal destiny through faith in the Lord Jesus. People are invited to receive the Lord (Jn. 1:12). Their freedom to decide is presupposed. They should not be forced by outward pressure to believe. If the Lord is standing at the door and knocks, waiting for it to be opened (Rev. 3:20), how should the state have the right to use force to try to impose the true faith?[33] It is of course altogether impossible for the state to impose any beliefs – it could only force people to outward conformity.

Brunner observed that spiritual freedom, the response of man to the voice of God, is not the same as freedom in a legal sense.[34] Spiritual freedom can also be experienced in prison or by a slave. The witness of so many Chinese Christians is an impressive example of this spiritual freedom.

This fact does not diminish the strong biblical arguments in favour of the recognition of freedom, both in a physical and mental sense. Human beings should have the possibility to decide, to make choices about the way they live. The state should not take over the primary responsibility of citizens for their own lives and the relationships between individuals in society. This principle of freedom is elaborated in several liberties, such as freedom of expression, freedom of assembly and freedom of association. We will concentrate here, however, on freedom of religion and belief as the freedom which was the first to be acknowledged.[35] It is, having regard to the Christian view of humanity, the most fundamental freedom. It is the recognition of not only the temporal but also the eternal destiny of man. In a sense it is also the freedom which is the most threatening to political power, because it recognises the possibility of a loyalty in human beings which may be stronger than their obedience to the state. In response to authorities which try to infringe upon Christians' obedience

---

[33]   Compare J.W. Montgomery, *Human Rights and Human Dignity*, *op. cit.*, n. 17 at 171.

[34]   Brunner, *Gerechtigkeit*, *op. cit.*, n. 27 at 66.

[35]   On freedom of religion see also Ian Leigh, 'Towards a Christian Approach to Religious Liberty', chapter 2 below.

to the Lord, only the answer of the apostles can be given that we ought to obey God rather than men (Acts 5:29).

The fundamental nature of this freedom was recognised when, long before the famous French Declaration of the Rights of Man and Citizen of 1789, religious liberty was proclaimed in the time of the Reformation. It was not just a pragmatic answer to the atrocities of the religious wars and persecutions of the sixteenth and seventeenth centuries. The plea for religious freedom was on the contrary the result of a return to the authority of the teachings of the Bible in the field of the relationship between church and state. It has been the great contribution of primarily the peaceful wing of the Anabaptist movement (as it was commonly called in those days) in the time of the Reformation to formulate and practise this biblical truth.[36] They stressed the personal character of their faith, the necessity of regeneration, the voluntary character of church membership and the separation of the church from the world in general and political power in particular. Already in 1554 the Frisian reformer Menno Simons (1496–1559) wrote that the church should not depend for its protection on political power. She could only be saved and protected by the Lord Jesus Christ with his powerful word and the Holy Spirit.[37] He referred to the parable of the wheat and the tares (Mt. 13:24–30) to explain that it is not up to the political authorities to sift between the true believers and the heretics.[38] A similar approach is found in the writings of the Baptist Roger Williams who is especially well known in the United States for his defence of religious freedom and of the separation of church and state. In his booklet *The Bloody Tenet of Persecution* (1644) he stated *inter alia* that:

> It is the will and command of God, that (since the coming of his Son the Lord Jesus) a permission of the most Paganish, Jewish, Turkish, or Antichristian consciences and worships, be granted to all men in all Nations and Countries: and that they are only to be fought against with that Sword which is only (in Soul matters) able to conquer, to wit, the Sword of God's Spirit, the Word of God . . .
>
> An inforced uniformity of Religion throughout a Nation or civil state confounds the Civil and Religious, denies the principles of Christianity and civility, and that Jesus Christ is come in the Flesh. . . .[39]

---

36 Compare also J.W. Allen, *A History of Political Thought in the Sixteenth Century*, (London, 1929), 35–48.

37 H.W. Meihuizen, *Menno Simons*, (Haarlem, 1961), 120. Compare also E.H. Broadbent, *The Pilgrim Church*, op. cit., n. 4 at 185–197.

38 M.C. Postema, *In het voetspoor van Menno Simonsz' gedachten*, (Kampen, 1986), 29–30; compare also Ronald J. Sider, 'An Evangelical Vision for American Democracy: An Anabaptist perspective', in *The Bible, Politics and Democracy*, (Grand Rapids, Michigan, 1987), 32–54, at 41.

39 Quoted from Leo Pfeffer, *Religious Freedom*, (Skokie, Illinois, 1979), 10–11.

In my view in line with the New Testament, Williams stresses the importance of the new phase in God's history we are in (compared to the Old Testament), by referring to the coming of God's Son to this world. This fact has as an important consequence the defence of religious freedom. There should be freedom to proclaim the gospel but also freedom for other religions and beliefs. This is not because of some sort of indifference to the truth, or a kind of middle-of-the-road humanism or polytheism which finds some truth in all beliefs, but because of the fact that it is not political force but only the Spirit of God by means of the Word of God which can convince. To this can be added what has been said before, namely that we cannot deny other people the freedom we should like to enjoy ourselves.

The ideas of Roger Williams were brought into practice in the colony of Rhode Island, which obtained in 1663 from King Charles II a Charter providing for religious freedom and the separation of church and state. This idea has since been accepted gradually by many Christians of different denominations and many non-Christians as well. It is surprising that the defence of toleration in the field of religion by John Locke is based on similar biblical arguments as we can learn from his *A Letter Concerning Toleration* (1689). Not reason and natural law, but the teaching of the New Testament, is the core of his argumentation. With regard to those in his day who tried to defend true religion by means of force he wrote the following:

> If like the Captain of our salvation, they sincerely desired the good of souls, they would tread in the steps and follow the perfect example of that Prince of peace, who sent out his soldiers to the subduing of nations, and gathering them into his church, not armed with the sword, or other instruments of force, but prepared with the Gospel of peace, and with the exemplary holiness of their conversation.[40]

Religious liberty implies, as we have seen, freedom to proclaim the gospel and as a consequence any message of a religious or non-religious nature. People should be free to adopt a religion or belief and to change their religion or belief. It is important to underline this in a world were there are many Islamic countries in which the change of religion or belief is severely punished.

Churches and other religious or non-religious organisations should be free to organise themselves according to their own principles. They should decide for themselves whether or not to ordain women in certain ministries, how to educate their ministers and to maintain their own disciplinary rules. Recognition of religious liberty should have as a consequence the separation of church and State.[41] This means that the

---

[40] John Locke, *A Letter Concerning Toleration*, Mario Montouri (ed.), (The Hague, 1963), 13.

[41] I am aware of the fact that this view is not shared by all Christian lawyers. See Julian Rivers, *Cambridge Paper on Religious Establishment*, (Vol. III,

State refrains from interference in the affairs of the church or other institutions related to religion or belief. Also the church and these other organisations should refrain from using political power to the benefit of their internal organisation. The church should not use the tax authorities to collect money from their members, as is the case in, for example, Germany or the Scandinavian countries. Of course the recognition of established churches does not mean automatically that there is no religious liberty. The United Kingdom is a clear and notable example of the combination of an established church and the recognition of religious liberty. Establishment may place the State as well as the church, however, in a difficult position. Political institutions are as such not competent to decide in spiritual matters, something they have to do in the case of an established church. They are not in a position to decide on the truth or falseness in the field of religion or belief. Should political authorities decide on who should lead the church? Are judges competent to decide on the proper interpretation of the Bible?

By way of clarification I should like to refer to a remarkable example from my own country concerning a small municipality in the Netherlands which is populated predominantly by Christians belonging to a variety of reformed, Calvinistic churches. The council of this municipality, which is the local government, is competent to make local by-laws. It created a by-law on subventions in which it provided that activities which were against the law of God could not receive a grant from the government. This rule has been quashed by the Crown as contrary to the freedom of religion and belief.[42] But imagine that it had remained in force and the following case would happen. A Seventh-Day Adventist requests a subsidy for the exploitation of his swimming pool, to be open every day of the week, except on the Sabbath, that is Saturday. The council of the municipality refuses the request because the opening of a swimming pool on Sundays was considered to be contrary to the law of God. Imagine the case being submitted to the District Court. How should it decide? Does a District Court know what the Word of God requires and how it should be interpreted? Should it follow the interpretation of the Seventh-Day Adventist or that of the municipal council? Or should it invite some experts from theological faculties?

The plea for the separation of church and state should not be misinter - preted as an argument to exclude believers in general or Christians in particular from participation in public debate or from activities in society.[43]

---

41 (continued)   No. 4). The differences seem to be due to diverging theological presuppositions concerning the relationship between the Old and the New Testaments and the position of the people of Israel and the church.

42 Koninklijk Besluit, 4 December 1984, Stb. 685, *Administratiefrechtelijke Beslissingen/NJ*, 1985, nr. 163.

43 Compare Ronald J. Sider, 'An Evangelical Vision for American Democracy: An Anabaptist Perspective' *op. cit.*, n. 38 at 41.

Unfortunately this mistake is quite common. In a study on religious pluralism and freedom of religion, Orlin expresses his concern about the influence of religious-inspired morality in legislation. [44] He criticises for example the European Court of Human Rights for its acceptance of the Irish divorce law, which reflects Roman Catholic morality in the case of *Johnston v Ireland*. [45] He is also concerned about religious influence on Polish abortion legislation. It does not require much imagination for this reason - ing to lead to the deprivation of political rights of believers, contrary to the principle of non-discrimination in the field of political rights. In this approach religious freedom becomes a device for the imposition of secular humanism as the state religion.

This is, however, not a correct interpretation. On the contrary, freedom of religion and belief implies freedom of conscience, the freedom to act according to one's religion or beliefs and to organise activities in society inspired by religion or belief. It is clear from the Bible that our faith should be a decisive factor for all aspects of our lives, not just the 'religious'. It should be underlined in this connection that there is not necessarily a tension between a biblical defence of religious freedom and the separation of church and state on the one hand and a biblical defence of, e.g., the protection of unborn life in a pluralist society, if we take into account the position of the church and Christians in society. While in Israel under the Old Testament there could be no question of separation of church and State, it is clear from the New Testament that the position of the church in the pluralist State is different. Both a restrictive attitude of the State in religious matters and the protection of human life by the law should be defended from a Christian point of view, as I have tried to explain in the preceding pages.

Of course not only in the field of politics, but also in other areas of society such as health care, charity and social work etc., the freedom to be active and establish institutions on the basis of one's religion or belief should be respected.

The State should refrain as much as possible from interference in this field. In practice this will not always be easy to realise. What is implied by respect for the consciences of citizens? In many countries conscientious objection against military service is recognised. The same is not true of similar objections against the obligation to pay taxes, or at least the part which will be spent on military purposes, as an English Quaker who went to the European Commission of Human Rights had to discover. [46] On

---

[44]   Compare Theodore S. Orlin, 'Religious Pluralism and Freedom of Religion: Its Protection in the Light of Church/State Relationships', in Alan Rosas and Jan Helgesen (eds.), *The Strength of Diversity: Human Rights and Pluralist Democracy*, (Dordrecht / Boston / London, 1992), 89–119.

[45]   Judgement of 22 October 1981, Publ. E.C.H.R., Series A, No. 45.

[46]   Case 10358/83, *C. v the United Kingdom*, Decisions and Reports (DR) 37, 142.

the other hand, recently the Dutch legislature introduced a provision in the civil code which protects to a certain extent workers who refuse to perform a specific task because of conscientious objections. [47]

Finally, the upbringing of children – their teaching and education – deserves special attention, when we discuss the freedom to live according to one's religion or belief in society. The State should not interfere with the upbringing of children in accordance with the convictions of the parents. This corresponds with the fundamental biblical notion of the relationship between parents and children. Parents should have the freedom to ensure their upbringing 'in the training and instruction of the Lord' (Eph. 6:4). Education and teaching are fundamental for the development of a person. It is clear that there does not exist something like 'neutral' knowledge which exists independently from fundamental presuppositions based on religion or belief. This should be recognised and therefore there should be freedom to provide for education and teaching explicitly based on such suppositions. This implies also that parents and private organisations have the right to establish schools on the basis of their religion and belief. This is recognised in Article 13 of the International Covenant on Economic, Social and Cultural Rights (New York, 1966). It is important of course that denominational schools and universities prove the reason for their existence by making clear that their teaching and education is fundamentally different from that provided for by the institutions which fall under the responsibility of the govern-ment. Unfortunately many schools and universities in my country which are denominational in name do not succeed in this. For that reason there is nowadays some criticism of the system in the Dutch constitution (Art. 23) which provides for not only the freedom to provide for education but also the financing of the system of denominational schools and universities by the state. *Noblesse oblige*!

V. Final Remarks

So far I have discussed some aspects of dignity, equality and freedom as basic values behind human rights in the light of the teaching of the Bible concerning humanity and its temporal and eternal destiny. It can be concluded that much can be said in favour of the respect for human rights from a Christian point of view. This respect can, however, never be unconditional. We have to bear in mind that our view of people and their destiny provides us also with a critical attitude towards dominant ideologies on human rights, which will frequently result in a different formulation and interpretation of these rights in practice. Therefore I have given some examples of the relevance of the discussion of the

[47] See Article 7: 681 para. 2 (e) Burgerlijk Wetboek (Civil Code).

Christian foundation of human rights for legal practice, which underlines the relevance of a specifically Christian perspective on the foundation of human rights, compared to other foundations.

In many other cases we appear to agree with others on both the formulation and the interpretation of human rights. This should not lead us to the conclusion that the discussion of a specific Christian foundation of human rights is irrelevant or even impossible. There are indeed authors who think a specific Christian idea of human rights or of morality in general is impossible.[48] This is clearly in contradiction with what is taught by the great number of biblical passages which deal explicitly with morality and underline the unique character of the contents as well as the motivation for moral behaviour of Christians compared to other people. This notwithstanding the fact that non-Christians also adhere to a number of biblical moral principles. This fact is recognised in the Bible itself. The unusual kindness of the pagan inhabitants of Malta is recorded (Acts 28:2), while Paul stresses that the Gentiles by nature do the things which are required by the law of God (Rom. 2:14). We should be thankful for this aspect of common grace. A minimum level of agreement on moral principles makes social life possible in a broken world. We are aware, however, that on many important issues there is no agreement on moral principles at all.

In this connection I should like to make one final remark. Years ago a representative of a student organisation approached me with a question on the interpretation of the Universal Declaration of Human Rights. He told me that formerly his organisation had been based on Christian principles. They had decided, however, to abolish these and to replace them by the Universal Declaration. He was therefore disturbed to find in the Universal Declaration a provision – Article 16, Paragraph 3 – which held that the family is the natural and fundamental group unit of society and that it is entitled to protection by society and the State. I guess the student was disturbed because it sounded so Christian, while the organ-isation wanted to get rid of its Christian background. This was a striking incident which is illustrative of two things. First it confirms that there is a considerable degree of agreement between human rights as they are formulated in the Universal Declaration and Christian moral principles. In the second place it illustrates a tendency which disturbs me, namely that human rights have for many people almost the significance of a religious belief, worthy to be included in the basic rules of an organisation. Human rights seem to have become the basis of a new creed. Similarly a Dutch humanist philosopher, Paul Cliteur, recently wrote that the

---

[48]   Compare Martin Honecker, *Das Recht des Menschen: Einführung in die evangelische Sozialethik*, (Gütersloh, 1978). He observes that there are no substantive Christian ethical principles for social life ('Es gibt keine besondere christliche Materialethik' at 25).

human rights tradition has since the Second World War become the first real world religion, albeit without God, church or rituals. [49] It is my view that Christians should not be found among the followers of this religion. They should not serve created things rather than God (Rom. 1:25), but instead remain where they are, outside the camp, seeking the city to come!

[49] Paul Cliteur, 'Maar nu, nu kunnen wij het moraliseren ook zelf', in Henk Peter Steenhuis (ed.), *Het debat over de moraal*, (Amsterdam, 1996), 13.

2

Towards a Christian Approach
to Religious Liberty

Ian Leigh[1]

I. Introduction

British Christians live in a political and cultural setting which has no direct biblical equivalent: a post-Christian, secular, multi-cultural soci‐ety. The formal arrangements of government continue to proclaim the establishment – the Church of England is the State church [2] – but for all practical purposes Christians of whatever denomination are a minority, one of a number of special interest groups tolerated within a liberal, secular society. Apart from religion, other poles of interest for such groups include sports, disability, environmental concern, sexual orien‐tation, ethnic origins, and so on. However, unlike other groups, religious groups are peculiarly likely to face bewildered non-recognition within a secular State because the all-embracing claims of religion to objective truth and to commitment from the believer sit ill alongside liberal toleration of minorities as *subjective* belief systems which are meaningful for those who hold them, but of no wider significance. Religion is acceptable to Liberals as *private* belief – freedom of con‐science – but can easily become questionable when it involves public demonstration (an approach which John Whitehead has characterised as 'the new pornography'). In particular, Liberal society cannot tolerate

[1] I gratefully acknowledge the assistance of my research assistant James Watson in locating many relevant materials and thank Colin Hart and Simon Calvert of the Christian Institute for discussing amendments to the Human Rights Bill with me. I am grateful also to Professor Paul Beaumont and to two anonymous referees who made helpful comments and suggestions on an earlier draft.

[2] In England. In Scotland the Church of Scotland is established: see F. Lyall, *Of Presbyters and Kings*, (Aberdeen, 1980), chs. 2–5; the Church of Wales was, however, disestablished by the Welsh Church Act 1914.

truth claims by one group which suggest that another minority's belief system or lifestyle is flawed. Nor do some Liberals easily recognise the contradiction within their own position – that for them toleration and subjectivity of truth have become unquestionable dogma (in this paper I call this 'Liberal Fundamentalism').

As a minority within an ostensibly liberal and tolerant society Christians have long enjoyed freedom within the law to worship, witness, evangelise and to live according to Jesus' teaching. This paper is concerned with developing a Christian approach to these civil liberties. This seems a particularly opportune time in which to reassess Christian approaches to religious liberty for two distinct reasons. First, the Liberal approach to freedom seems itself to have reached a crisis of sorts in what is fashionably termed 'political correctness'. In their insistence on a particular interpre - tation of equal opportunities regardless of race, religion, sex and sexual orientation, some North American exponents of political correctness have found little space for freedom of speech for others whose views they or any other 'minority' find offensive – especially religious groups making absolute truth claims or espousing objective morality (frequently, on the topics of abortion and homosexuality). One way to understand this paradox is that in the perpetual sibling rivalry between liberty and equality the latter has gained the upper hand. Political correctness of this type has made a substantial inroad into public bodies (not least universities) in Britain, many of whom have formal equal opportunities documents subscribing to such values, and in the media, where alternative voices are seldom given space. Where education and the media lead, the law is often found not far behind. In this instance, however, the incorporation of the European Convention on Human Rights into British law may also provide religious groups with added protection in a climate which is increasingly hostile, in the shape of Article 9 (see p. 60 for the text), giving for the first time a positive right in British law of freedom of thought, belief and religion.

In the discussion which follows there is first an introductory attempt to elucidate key themes in Liberal approaches to religious liberty and to identify some of the problems which have emerged with these ap - proaches, both in terms of internal consistency and by way of external critique. The following section makes a similar attempt to elucidate Christian approaches to religious liberty. The second half of the paper considers two vexed questions by way of case studies: the law of blasphemy and the incorporation of a right to freedom of religion through the Human Rights Bill.

II. Liberalism and Religious Liberty

In this section Liberalism is used to refer to a cluster of related beliefs and theories within moral and political philosophy concerning morality, the individual and the State.[3] As a matter of history the rise of Liberal thought was closely connected with the growth of religious toleration, but although religious toleration and religious liberty remain important issues of debate for liberalism, they could no longer be described as a central concern. Modern forms of Liberalism are infinitely varied and so secreted within popular thinking (especially through notions of pluralism and relativism) they can scarcely be disentangled from many innate patterns of modern thought. However, I will first attempt to sketch some persistent themes for this discussion. The account is necessarily impres - sionistic and it will soon become apparent some Liberals do not share all the characteristics described.

In understanding how Liberals approach religious belief and experience a fundamental distinction in categorising knowledge is that traceable to David Hume: a distinction between subjective and objective truth (the so-called 'fact–value' distinction). In his *Treatise on Human Nature* Hume argued that matters of morality were firmly within the realm of subjec - tivity and, hence, incapable of final proof or resolution. Hume famously connected this with different forms of discussion – 'is' and 'ought' – in his deductive fallacy. Consigning religious belief and experience to the subjective realm is a persistent attitude not only in popular thought but also among Liberal intellectuals. Liberals have considerable difficulty in understanding, still less accommodating, claims of absolute truth by people who they label as 'true believers' or 'fundamentalists'.

The subjective nature of morality and religion for Liberals has implica - tions for how they view the actions and responsibilities of individuals. Respect for individual autonomy in moral matters is a cornerstone of Liberalism. It is on this basis that thinkers in a line which runs from Socrates through Thoreau to John Stuart Mill have argued that it is impermissible for the State to interfere in matters of individual conscience and that should it attempt to do so the individual has a right (or, in some theories, a duty) to resist. In the case of religious freedom some writers have argued not merely that it is impermissible for the State to interfere in individual choices, but also that it is counter-productive or impracticable. John Locke made the point vividly in his *A Letter Concerning Toleration* where he argued that a church was a voluntary society, and that it was beyond the power of civil authorities to coerce individuals in matters of belief, since faith was

---

[3]   Readers versed in political philosophy will notice that I do not at this point distinguish between 'anti-perfectionist' and 'perfectionist' Liberals. From an external viewpoint the difference is less apparent than it is to insiders for reasons that I explain in the treatments of Rawls and Raz below.

For a more systematic overview of the different strands of Liberalism – from constitutional liberalism, to classical economic liberalism and welfare liberalism, focusing on Locke, Kant, Mill, Hobhouse and Hayek, see R. Song, *Christianity and Liberal Theory*, (Oxford, 1997), ch. 2.

only effective if freely arrived at and genuinely held.[4] These views are obviously closely connected with the protestant emphasis on personal moral responsibility, individual salvation and the importance of a personal response and commitment to God. Liberal attitudes towards individual autonomy may, however, clash with such belief systems, for example, with regard to the approach they would take on religious education and upbringing of children, who may be treated as autonomous individuals by Liberals earlier (or later) than they are by their parents.[5]

A third characteristic of Liberal attitudes towards religion is a position of professed 'neutrality'. According to this view, religious belief is a 'private' matter for individuals and something which the State should not interfere with in the public domain. Classically, the 'privatisation' of religion is expressed in the First Amendment to the United States' Constitution: 'Congress shall make no law respecting an establishment of religion, or prohibiting the free exercise thereof . . .' Similarly, the Australian constitution provides:

> Commonwealth shall not make any law for establishing any religion, or for imposing any religious observance, or for prohibiting the free exercise of any religion, and no religious test should be required as a qualification of any office or public trust under the Commonwealth.[6]

Neutrality therefore implies a withdrawal of State competence within matters of private conscience, mirroring the emphasis on individual autonomy and the subjective nature of religious belief according to Liberals.

Fourthly, Liberals acknowledge the importance of freedom for individuals to change their religious beliefs. This is both an aspect of individual autonomy and also goes to the very heart of why Liberals think the protection of personal freedom and freedom of expression is worthwhile. One of the major justifications in classical Liberal thought has always been that they enable individuals to pursue their own conception of the truth. J.S. Mill advances this as a justification for freedom of expression in *On Liberty*. Likewise, Locke in his *A Letter Concerning Toleration* argues that no-one is born into a particular church but must decide for themselves on matters of religious belief, which is a question which cannot be determinately settled by any human authority on an individual's behalf.

---

[4]   Locke enjoys an ambiguous status for the purpose of this discussion. He is undoubtedly a constitutional liberal (that is, an exponent of limited government based, in his case, on a social contractarian theory of natural rights) as exemplified in *The Two Treatises on Government*. However, there is much both in the theological grounding of his natural rights and in his theological defence of religious liberty (see the discussion of the *Letter Concerning Toleration* below) which I wish to adopt as an example of a Christian position.

[5]   In a different sphere this was substantially the issue in *Gillick* v *W. Norfolk and Wisbech Health Authority* [1986] AC 112.

[6]   Commonwealth of Australia Act 1900, s.116.

A final feature of Liberal approaches is intolerance of religious intolerance or dogmatism. Following the subjective/objective distinction
described above, Liberals view any attempt to practice or express religious
belief outside the confines of subjective thought and experience with
suspicion and hostility. Claims that religious truth is objective or universal
are, paradoxically, the one type of religious expression which Liberals
cannot tolerate. This explains, for example, long-standing Liberal hostility
to the existence of blasphemy laws [7] and the Liberal response to Muslim
outrage following the publication of Salman Rushdie's book *The Satanic
Verses*.

John Rawls offers a developed defence of this position in his *A Theory
of Justice*.[8] He argues in a section entitled 'Toleration of the Intolerant':

> . . . from the standpoint of the original position, no particular interpretation
> of religious truth can be acknowledged as binding upon citizens generally;
> nor can it be agreed that there can be one authority with the right to settle
> questions of theological doctrine. Each person must insist upon an equal right
> to decide what his religious obligations are. He cannot give up this right to
> another person or institutional authority. In fact, a man exercised his liberty
> in deciding to accept that another has an authority even when he regards this
> authority as infallible, since in doing this he in no way abandons his equal
> liberty of conscience as a matter of constitutional law. For this liberty as
> secured by justice is imprescriptible: a person is always free to change his faith
> and this right does not depend upon his having exercised his powers of choice
> regularly and intelligently. We may observe that men's having an equal liberty
> of conscience is consistent with the idea that all men ought to obey God and
> accept the truth. The problem of liberty is that of choosing a principle by
> which the claims men make on one another in the name of their religion are
> to be regulated. Granting that God's will should be followed and the truth
> recognised does not as yet define a principle of adjudication. From the fact
> that God's intention is to be complied with it does not follow that any person
> or institution has the authority to interfere with another's interpretation of his
> religious obligations. This religious principle justifies no-one in demanding
> in law or politics a greater liberty for himself. The only principles which
> authorize claims on institutions are those that would be chosen in the original
> position.

Having established the case for toleration Rawls argues that an 'intolerant
sect' is not entitled to complain if it is not itself tolerated within a State
since a complaint is only justified and in good faith when according to
principles shared by the complainant and the person to whom it is
addressed. However:

> While an intolerant sect does not itself have title to complain of intolerance,
> its freedom should be restricted only when the tolerant society sincerely and

---

[7] See pp. 52–59 below.
[8] *A Theory of Justice*, (Oxford, 1971), 216–221.

with reason believe that their own security and that of the institutions of liberty are in danger.[9]

Other people may be justified, according to Rawls, in invoking the principles of justice to require equal treatment of intolerant sects, how - ever, its adherents are themselves disqualified from doing so. Neverthe - less, he argues that it is proper to 'force the intolerant to respect the liberty of others, since a person can be required to respect the rights established by principles that he would acknowledge in the original position'. Beyond this, however, the existence of a 'just constitution' (i.e. respecting basic liberties according to Rawls' own theory) should be sufficient safeguard against intolerant minorities; he even argues that the enjoyment of such liberties under the constitution may in time lead the intolerant towards a belief in freedom.

The deep-rooted and all-embracing character of Rawls' views on justice is apparent in his *Theory of Justice*. He plainly envisages religious and moral convictions as being essentially subservient and secondary to principles of justice.[10] He argues that where those convictions conflict with the principles which people would choose in his 'original position', the latter principles will override, and claims that 'the principles of justice can adjudicate between opposing moralities just as they regulate the claims of rival religions'.[11] It is apparent from this formulation that principles of justice and consistency are somehow more fundamental than religious belief. Indeed, we may go further and say that for advocates like Rawls these principles have taken the position that religious belief enjoys for others – that is, they are the most serious and important truths which they hold.[12]

---

9   *Ibid.*, at 220.
10   Indeed, this subservience is schematised in Rawls' thought, since his indi-
     viduals in the 'original position' are deprived of (*inter alia*) their own religious
     convictions behind a 'veil of ignorance' for the purpose of choosing neutral
     principles of justice.
11   *Idem.*
12   In later work, however, Rawls has attempted to meet criticisms by offering
     an 'anti-perfectionist' reinterpretation of his theory in which justice as
     fairness is offered as no more than the best public justification of the value
     of a political community to its citizens: J. Rawls, *Political Liberalism*, (New
     York, 1993), especially ch. 1. There Rawls argues that the veil of ignorance
     is a 'device of representation' (27) and that justice as fairness implies 'no
     metaphysical doctrine' (29). Purportedly, this version of the theory does not
     rely on advancement of Liberal values as objectively good. Nevertheless, it
     is premised on what Rawls treats to be sociological facts – that pluralism is
     a permanent feature of modern society and that disagreements among people
     about conceptions of the good are reasonable, leading some commentators
     to argue that even in this form his theory is based on a type of scepticism

In the discussion which follows criticism of Liberal approaches to freedom of religion is advanced from two quite different perspectives, first an external viewpoint which is radically critical of Liberal claims of neutrality and, secondly, with regard to their internal consistency and application.

External critiques of Liberalism

The discussion of Rawls alerts us to the fact that religious belief is something essentially foreign and incomprehensible to Liberals. [13] Liberals can only understand religious belief within their own framework of beliefs, and this necessarily subordinates religion: in the secondary position it is acceptable and understandable as a matter of personal and subjective belief, outside these confines it is suspect and even dangerous. Marshall quotes Rawls: 'to subordinate all our aims to one end . . . strikes as irrational, or more likely as mad'. [14] An argumentative strategy in which Liberal intellectuals resort to the academic equivalent of playground name-calling is revealing.

This subordination and detachment from whole-hearted religious commitment is also reflected strikingly (and paradoxically) by the most prominent of modern natural lawyers, John Finnis. [15] For Finnis religion (which, on his definition, would include atheism) is one of seven 'objective goods' which individuals combine and rank in order to form a coherent life plan. However, his requirements of 'practical reasonable-ness' stipulate that it is unwise either to ignore any of the objective goods arbitrarily or to give priority to any one of them to the exclusion of others. This then is a natural law theory firmly within the Liberal mould. Finnis argues that we should regard any project pursued as part of the life plan with a certain detachment. Contrast with Jesus' claim that 'whoever loses his life for my sake will find it' (Mt. 10:39), the call to the first disciples to leave everything and follow him (Mt. 4:18–22) and to the rich young ruler to sell all his possessions and give to the poor and then follow him (Mt. 19:21) could not be more striking. The Liberal predisposition towards detachment follows naturally from the emphasis upon individual autonomy: the autonomous individual risks *losing control* of his or her life by making long-term or far-reaching commitments based on religious conviction. This contrasts directly with Jesus' claim that true freedom is to be found in whole-hearted obedience to him.

---

12 *(continued)* and is perhaps less anti-perfectionist than Rawls claims: S. Mulhall and A. Swift, *Liberals and Communitarians*, (Oxford, 1992), at 184–5 and 222–5.

13 Cf. P. Marshall, *Their Blood Cries Out*, (Word, Texas, 1997), at 188–190.

14 *Ibid.*, at 189.

15 *Natural Law and Natural Rights*, (Oxford, 1980), 89 and 109–110.

At the same time Liberals are unable to understand the nature of religious controversy; this leads, for example, to Rawls' naive claim that justice can act as an arbiter between religions. A detached observer might, for example, think rival football supporters are united by a common interest in football, but this is the kind of statement which could only be made by someone with a relative lack of interest in the game. In a sense true, it nevertheless totally fails to understand two opposing positions. Liberals can only succeed in reconciling mutually contradictory religious claims by stifling or diluting them in a way which they may find convincing but which the adherents will not. It follows that within a Liberal society there is a permanent tension between the State and those advancing claims based on religious conviction.

However, arguably there is a further problem with Liberalism's pro - fession of neutrality – its claim to detachment. Since Liberals are prepared to tolerate other beliefs only within their own framework of under - standing, this appears to contradict Liberalism's own espoused principles of neutrality. The fervour and conviction with which Liberalism is held by some of its advocates suggests that it is appropriate to turn the tables and suggest that what is at stake is 'Liberal Fundamentalism', itself a dogmatic system of thought held with the tenacity of religious belief. In its privileging of this Liberalism the Liberal State violates both the espoused principles of separation of religion from the State and of non-discrimination.

One of the foremost contemporary Liberal theorists, Joseph Raz, both illustrates and openly confronts a number of these points in his work. In *The Morality of Freedom*[16] he argues for a perfectionist Liberalism: one which recognises the value of autonomy but which suggests that the State should not be neutral but should actively encourage (though not through coercive means) certain forms of the good life. Raz argues that in doing so Liberals are not overruling the beliefs of others nor coercing them, nor is the State endorsing a single 'acceptable' vision of life to the exclusion of alternatives. The implications for religious freedom are spelled out in a later work where he addresses the controversy raised over the Rushdie affair and confronts the difficulties of intolerance: [17]

> Strong pluralism of this kind finds itself, as the Rushdie case illustrates, approving as valuable, though imperfect, ways of life which themselves deny the truth of pluralism. Of course the anti-pluralistic views which underlie such ways of life are regarded as wrong, and the ways of life that they inform are correspondingly imperfect. They are rival ways of life, but none the less recognised as valuable. . . .
>
> Where a dominant pluralistic outlook leads to the recognition of rival ways of life, conflict is inevitable. The pluralist, while finding value in ways of life

16   (Oxford, 1986).
17   J. Raz, *Ethics in the Public Domain*, (rev. ed., Oxford, 1994), 164–167.

informed by some wrong beliefs, must inevitably differ from people who have those wrong beliefs about what precisely is valuable in their lives and why.[18]

He then proceeds to argue that the consequence is that pluralists can without inconsistency accept the 'value' of anti-pluralist ways of life without being committed to approving and supporting all aspects of them: 'Because it recognises the value of ways of life which it (partly) disagrees with, pluralism is committed to a society in which conflicting ideologies are accepted, and tolerated.'[19]

A number of features of this approach are commendably frank: Raz recognises that different religious views are 'rival' views and that the rivalry extends to '[D]isagreement, condemnation and even hostility to certain aspects of rival ways of life';[20] he freely admits also that pluralism is itself a similar rival way of life, rather than a 'neutral' position based on general scepticism or abandonment of judgement. This very clarity points up the difference in outlook. For Raz, Christianity and Islam are rival ways but not incompatible, in the sense that a Christian and a Muslim may approve of aspects of each other's lives, while strongly disagreeing with other aspects or beliefs. An atheist may 'value' a Christian's life because it is informed by respect for human beings or aesthetic sensibility. Raz is arguing openly and clearly for a dominant pluralist outlook on such differences and towards the value in alternative ways of life. The Muslim and the Christian might, after all, argue that the aspects of each other's lives that they respect are trivial in the overall schemes of their conflicting beliefs and that it is only through a pluralist viewpoint that both can be seen to have value. Moreover, Raz consciously uses the concept of 'value' to privilege pluralism: a way of life is valuable for him because it is freely chosen from the alternatives available, even if it is anti-pluralist. The 'value' for the believer will, of course, be quite different but Raz's Liberalism does not commit him to giving recognition to that perspective.

Few writers on law and religion recognise or confront the difficulty over their chosen commentary point openly. However, two authors, Bradney and Unsworth, deserve honourable mention. In his study of religious liberty in Britain, Bradney bases his critical analysis of the law squarely and openly on the principle of 'radical autonomy of the individual'.[21] This approach has the merit that the foundations are explicit and can be accepted or rejected by the reader; few other legal authors are either so self-aware or open in declaring their preconceptions. Unsworth for his part in writing about blasphemy is also explicit in recognising the difficulty:

[18] *Ibid.*, at 166.
[19] *Ibid.*, at 167.
[20] *Ibid.*, at 166.
[21] A. Bradney, *Religions, Rights and Laws*, (Leicester, 1993), ch. 2.

that once a relativistic perspective is admitted, then the secular democratic liberal humanism which has been the dominant ideological force shaping policy in response to pluralism, rather than providing an overarching framework for arbitration, is itself reduced to the status of but another enclosed discourse, unable to engage with Islamic or Christian claims other than in its own patently subordinating terms.[22]

The criticisms in this section have been based on an external viewpoint – one sceptical of Liberalism's claims. However, we should also consider arguments from within Liberalism itself. For, even if the basic approaches to religious liberty outlined earlier are accepted, their application and scope reveal further difficulties, to which we now turn.

Internal critiques of Liberal approaches to religious freedom

In this section four difficulties are discussed: the tension between claims of State detachment and equality in delineating which religious practices are worthy of protection; underlying difficulties in defining religions; and the problems of clashing freedom, both between freedom of religion and other liberties, and among those claiming mutually inconsistent protections for their religious belief and practice. The first two questions are essentially definitional, the latter two arise in the practical application of freedom of religion. All, however, may lead to inconsistencies in practice.

First, there may be difficulties of internal consistency, between the claims of State detachment and equality arising from this supposed neutrality. Sadurski has analysed the apparent conflict arising from Lib - eralism's professed neutrality between definitions of religion under the 'Non-Establishment' and 'Free Exercise' principles applicable to the US and Australian Constitutions.[23] He argues that whereas the dynamic of the Free Exercise principle is to encourage an expansive definition of religion (because of the dangers of adopting a bias against putative religions), that of the Non-Establishment principle is restrictive, because the effect of the principle is to invalidate State action within contested spheres. If an attempt is made to maintain a consistent approach between these different concerns the result is confusion:

> the more general the concept of religion is under the Free Exercise Principle, the less effective the Non-Establishment Principle becomes in determining the sphere of permissible, secular State action.[24]

---

[22]   C. Unsworth, 'Blasphemy, Cultural Divergence and Legal Relativism', [1995] 58, *Modern Law Review*, 658 at 659.

[23]   W. Sadurski, 'On Legal Definitions of "Religion" ', (1989), 63 *Australian Law Journal*, 834. For the relevant texts see p. 34 above.

[24]   Sadurski, *op. cit.*, n. 23 at 840.

Sadurski argues that the conflict can be reconciled by an appeal to the overarching Liberal idea of 'the State's neutrality between religions, and also between religious and non-religious moral conceptions'.[25]

The two principles give effect to neutrality in different ways: the Free Exercise principle provides that choice of religion does not affect the legal rights which an individual possesses, whereas the Non-Establishment principle entails the disengagement of the State from religious bodies in order to ensure equality (it is linked with the Liberal view which confines religion to the private sphere). Accordingly, Sadurski argues, that whereas definitional exactitude is required for the Non-Establishment principle, since it is necessary for the boundary between the public and private spheres to be clear, it is unnecessary in the case of the Free Exercise principle. Here the main use of a definition of religion is to distinguish between religious and other moral convictions, whereas Sadurski con-tends that 'the distinction is . . . . of no importance, because the wrong committed through illegitimate State coercion consists in restricting one's moral choice'.[26]

Sadurski has performed a valuable service in identifying clearly some of the conflicting trends within the approaches of Liberal States to religion. However, his attempt to rescue the project faces problems of its own. These derive from its own Liberal frame of reference. He employs a distinction between the public and private spheres to justify a difference in approach between the two principles. However, the distinction is only really convincing when the viewpoint is a constitu-tional one involving solely questions of State action. The difficulty becomes apparent when we consider the status of private action which discriminates against another person on grounds of their religion, or attempts to coerce them in matters of religion. Modern examples might include discrimination over religious dress in employment or education; older examples concern restrictive covenants barring certain religious groups from use of land or testators who attempt to influence their beneficiaries' choice of religion. The public/private distinction and the 'Free Exercise' rights can be used to justify directly contradictory approaches to private action of this kind. Plainly, if the discrimination is permitted by law it can be explained as falling within the private sphere where the law ought not to interfere with individual choices: it may even be regarded as a valid exercise of the discriminator's own 'Free Exercise' rights. Conversely, if the discrimination is prevented this can be explained as protection of the victim's 'Free Exercise' rights and/or by regarding discrimination on religious grounds as an impermissible

---

[25]   *Idem*. Neutrality entails, according to Sadurski: 'that no legal burden or privilege can attach to an individual's choice, change and pursuit of religious ideals (nor the choice of a non-religious morality).'

[26]   *Ibid.*, at 841.

factor outside the protected private sphere of choices.[27] Moreover, if as a result of the public/private distinction the law is simultaneously engaged in prohibiting *State* behaviour where the effect is to discriminate on grounds of religion, but permitting it in the case of a private actor, the legal message is at best confused and, arguably, inconsistent.

Sadurski's attempt to abandon definitional difficulties is also problematic. The protection for moral convictions is fully in line with Liberal respect for individuals as morally autonomous agents and the view that it is impermissible for the State to interfere with such choices by preference for one vision of morality over another. However, some boundary is still required to the Free Exercise principle, unless the position is taken that any claim by an individual to be morally bound according to the individual's own beliefs deserves respect and freedom of exercise. Defining the limits of 'morality' suffers many of the same pitfalls as defining 'religion'.

The second internal difficulty – the more general problem of defining what constitutes religion, for the purpose of protection – is one of the most frequently recurring themes in the legal literature on freedom of religion.[28] Most writers wish to cast the net as widely as possible, and are suspicious of traditional categories of religion. On the other hand, some limitation is required, especially because of the rights claimed for free exercise of religion.

It can be argued that Liberal neutrality requires not merely neutrality between religions but also neutrality between religious convictions and other political and moral beliefs such as pacifism, vegetarianism, environmentalism, and so on. In such a scheme the freedom protected is not so much that of a particular belief system as that of the individual to believe whatever he or she chooses. Some writers on religious liberty see this as a means by which to escape difficulties over what should count as a religion for the purpose of religious freedom. Ibán argues that it provides a way for European legal thought to move beyond categories of legal protection based in the main on the historical influence of traditional religions, towards full legal recognition and acceptance of the practices of new sects:

> . . . the expected movement towards the achievement of complete religious
> . neutrality cannot consist in the simple consideration that all religions deserve
> protection. What should . . . be protected, in a system of equality, is the

---

[27]   The two are not the same: a private individual's conduct may satisfy some principle of non-discrimination although his action impacts equally on people of different religious views, and hence, prevents 'Free Exercise' by all of them.

[28]   For a recent example see C. Hall, 'Aggiornamento: Reflections Upon the Contemporary Legal Concept of Religion', (1996), 27 *Cambrian Law Review* 6.

legitimate expression of individual free will on all matters. In other words what should be protected is not one religion, nor all religions, but rather the individual who believes . . .

. . . namely protection of free exercise of any option (of thought, religion, politics, etc.), without classification of this option and with the only limitation being respect for what are deemed to be essential values.[29]

However, the difficulty in according recognition to an individual's beliefs arises not principally as regards belief but rather the limits to permissible *manifestation* of that belief, especially where it affects other people; any legal system would still need some means of differentiating which beliefs are important enough to be respected by non-interference, despite the fact that the exercise of them may have some non-consensual impact on other people which they dislike or consider harmful.

In somewhat similar vein Peter Edge has argued in the context of discussing protection for freedom of religion under Article 9 that the European Court of Human Rights should prefer justifications for freedom of religion based on individual personal development and individual 'self-definition' to those based on social considerations (such as recogni - tion of religious diversity and encouraging all groups to feel part of society).[30] This, he argues, is more likely to afford protection for very small religious minorities. Edge recognises, however, that this requires some distinction to be drawn between 'convictions' (i.e. core beliefs) and the right to hold and act on personal opinions, with reference to 'the centrality of the belief or conviction to the individual's definition, and construction, of their own personality'.[31] This is similar to the so-called 'subjective-functional' approach adopted by the US Supreme Court in a line of cases following *Seeger* v *US*.[32]

[29] I.C. Ibán, 'Religious Toleration and Freedom in Continental Europe', (1997), 10 *Ratio Juris* 90 at 105.

[30] P.W. Edge, 'Current Problems in Article 9 of the European Convention of Human Rights', (1996), *Juridical Review* 42, 47–50; see also P. Edge, 'The Legal Challenges of Paganism and Other Diffuse Faiths', [1996] 1 *Journal of Civil Liberties*, 216.

[31] *Current Problems*, 49–50. From the external perspective of orthodox Christian belief an obvious difficulty with this approach arises from the way in which it pushes individual autonomy arguments to their full extent – quite literally, self-centredness – a view in which the universe revolves around the individual's beliefs. This sits ill alongside Christian notions of the sovereignty of God and the legitimate Lordship of Christ: if God is sovereign he defines humanity, not vice versa. The argument therefore goes considerably further than the need to respect and protect freedom of choice in matters of belief, which I argue for below.

[32] 380 US 163 (1965); see further Hall, *op. cit.*, n. 28 at 25ff.

Quite apart from definitional problems, Liberal support for freedom of religion also faces the difficulty of conflicting rights. The same concern for individual autonomy and State neutrality as regards visions of the good life leads Liberals to support a number of other rights, especially, freedom of speech, privacy and equality. One has only to consider the problems of the law of blasphemy (explored more fully below) or of the ordination of women or of homosexuals to realise that it is contradictory to pursue all such claims as equally valid – at some point the law will have to ascribe a higher value to one than another, and where this occurs the subordinate right is qualified as a result. This dilemma provokes reflection among Liberals about which right is more fundamental; for example, in a recent essay Mullally has used Gewirth's Principle of Generic Consistency to construct an argument for giving priority to sex equality over freedom of religion.[33] The European Court of Human Rights, on the other hand, in upholding the validity of blasphemy laws (notably in the *Otto-Preminger Institute* case, considered below) has given priority to freedom of religion over freedom of expression. Recent attempts to amend the Human Rights Bill to protect certain aspects of freedom of conscience[34] can also be interpreted as an attempt to give priority to freedom of religion over other rights.

The problem of clashing rights is not, however, merely an issue in considering the relative status of freedom of religion and other rights; it can also arise between two individuals, each basing themselves on freedom of religion, especially where one finds another's views offensive or threatening. The European Court of Human Rights faced this issue squarely in the case of *Kokkanakis* v *Greece*[35] in which a Jehovah's Witness successfully challenged his prosecution for the offence of unlawful proselytism as a violation of Article 9. The court held that evangelism was within the protected activities under the Article, but some statements in the judgements show that there are clear limitations, designed to

---

[33]   S. Mullally, 'Beliefs that Discriminate: A rights-based Solution?', in C. Gearty and A. Tomkins (eds.), *Understanding Human Rights*, (London, 1996), 480–506. The implications for voluntary associations like churches remain slightly unclear: Mullally argues that application of Gewirth's approach requires the State to recognise freedom of religion embracing discriminatory practices only to the extent that such bodies demonstrate *true* voluntariness among those joining (*ibid.*, at 501). The obvious rejoinder that State interference is not justified if dissenting members have the option of forming a separate and non-discriminatory religious body of their own, which would be equally recognised under the law, is not explored.

[34]   pp. 64–70 below.

[35]   (1993), 17 E.H.R.R. 397; for analysis see P. Edge, 'The Missionary's Position after *Kokkanakis* v *Greece*', [1995] 2 *Web Journal of Current Legal Issues*; C. Hamilton, *Family, Law and Religion*, (London, 1995), at 26–29.

protect others from being brow-beaten or taken advantage of, which the majority also based on freedom of thought. The Greek law was found to violate Article 9 because it covered not only 'improper proselytism' but also legitimate manifestation of religious beliefs. In proposing a distinction between proper and improper proselytism (which is not elucidated clearly in the majority opinions), with the suggestion that the State can take sides in religious controversy to criminalise the latter, the majority judgements raise serious doubts about the neutrality of the State in defending freedom of religion under the Convention. Whilst there might be common agreement that techniques such as force and brainwashing are impermis - sible, critics of public evangelism who approach religious belief from an essentially privatised perspective sometimes argue that any public discus - sion which is couched in rhetorical terms and which the hearer might find distressing infringes the other's rights.[36] A similar attitude of mind is present in some judicial comments in *Kokkanakis*, especially the dissenting judges, who would have held that a ban on all proselytism did not violate Article 9.[37] This attitude treats religious belief as private and subjective territory, where public manifestation of belief is less valued than cerebral and detached exploration of the questions involved. But it plainly undervalues the freedom of speech of the speaker and the autonomy of the hearer, to which Liberals ought also to be committed. This was recognised by Judge Martens in a partly dissenting judgement in which he argued that it was impermissible for the State to take on the role of policing religious controversy and that arguments of human autonomy and freedom of expression militated against State interference in attempts by one person to convince another to change religion.[38]

[36] An attitude of this kind underlies a ban on broadcast evangelism imposed by the Independent Television Commission on non-satellite and cable televi-sion broadcasters in the United Kingdom: see I. Leigh, 'Regulating Relig-ious Broadcasting', (1992), 10 *Ecclesiastical Law Journal*, 287–304 discussing the Broadcasting Act 1990 and related Codes of Practice.

[37] See especially Judge Valticos: 'This is a far cry from merely manifesting one's belief, as covered by Article 9. Someone who proselytises seeks to convert others; he does not confine himself to affirming his faith but seeks to change that of others to his own'; later in the same passage he writes of 'rape of the beliefs of others' (17 European Human Rights Reports [EHRR] 430). See also Joint Dissenting Opinion of Judges Foighel and Loizon: 'One cannot be deemed to show respect for the rights and freedom of others if one employs means that are intended to entrap someone and dominate his mind in order to convert him' (17 EHRR 439).

[38] '. . . the State being, bound to strict neutrality in religious matters . . . should not set itself as the arbiter for assessing whether particular religious behaviour is "proper" or "improper" . . . is lacking intrinsic justification for attributing greater value to the freedom not to be proselytised than the right to

III. Towards a Christian Approach

Many of the emphases of Liberalism discussed above are traceable historically to Christian writers and thinkers, especially those in the seventeenth century, who laid the foundation for modern Liberalism. The religious conflicts of that age were the backdrop against which ideas of religious toleration were developed from Christian foundations, espe - cially by John Locke in his *A Letter Concerning Toleration*. The recognition of freedom to practice one's beliefs in public, to change religions, and toleration of religious minorities are all derived from these concerns. Freedom of religion preceded many of the other civil liberties now routinely claimed within Liberal States, although in the case of Britain the legal implementation of the ideal of religious toleration was slow and tortuous, and in some respects is not yet complete more than three centuries after Locke wrote.[39]

A number of the foundational beliefs of Liberalism identified earlier can be traced via this route to distinctively Christian, or at least Protestant, ideas. The doctrine of the priesthood of all believers militated against the assumption by any human authority – whether within the church or State – of the power to determine with finality matters of religious controversy. This was a cornerstone of Locke's argument[40] and finds a clear echo in Rawls' insistence that even if we accept that God's will is clear and to be complied with, no individual or institution has *locus standi* to 'interfere with another's interpretation of his religious obligations'.[41] However, this doctrine is held in tension with the duty laid by Jesus on all believers to tell others of their beliefs and the authority of Scripture as the Word of God by which the individual and the church can distinguish truth and error. The New Testament contains many clear examples of believers using Scripture to rebuke and correct fellow believers, either in person or through letters, to persuade non-believers and to justify their actions and beliefs before religious and secular authorities. All of this suggests that whatever a Christian approach to toleration may mean, it does not entail a silent acceptance of conflicting beliefs in the name of pluralism.

Locke argues for toleration of people whose beliefs he regards as *wrong*. Toleration, however, did not disable even a ruler from attempting to persuade (but not to coerce) others of truth in matters of belief.[42] Locke's case for toleration is quite different from that advanced by Liberals from

---

[38] *(continued)* proselytise . . .' (17 EHRR 437). Similarly Judge Pettiti in a Partly Concurring Opinion argued that freedom of religion under Article 9 extended to what the majority had labelled 'improper' proselytism (*ibid.*, at 426).

[39] On the development of religious toleration see: St John Robilliard, *Religion and the Law*, (Manchester, 1984), Appendix; Hamilton, *op. cit.*, n. 35, ch. 1.

[40] For example, see J. Horton and S. Mendus (eds.), *John Locke: A Letter Concerning Toleration in Focus*, (London, 1991), at 18 and 50–1.

[41] *A Theory of Justice*, 218.

[42] Horton and Mendus, *op. cit.*, n. 40 at 18–19.

Mill onwards: the argument is grounded not on scepticism, which sees toleration as important because of the impossibility of arriving at finality in religious belief, nor on the case for diversity, which sees belief as a commodity in the marketplace – the wider the choice the better. Rather, the argument is based primarily on pragmatic grounds – religious perse - cution is *ineffective*. The means available to the State only concern outward compulsion of the person and this can never produce genuine belief. Some have therefore criticised Locke for failing to provide a moral argument against religious persecution. [43]

For Christians an attractive feature of Locke's case is the central importance which he accords to personal belief in his defence of tolera - tion. This, however, means that he gives lesser prominence to protection of other manifestations of religious belief. He would allow restrictions on religious practice to be imposed for non-religious reasons (for example, public health reasons in the case of animal sacrifice) and he provides no guidance on the weight to be given to the two considerations. Locke is, after all, one Christian writing for other Christians (including rulers) in the context of a society which is outwardly at least predominantly Christian, giving reasons why religious persecution on religious grounds is indefensible. Although he was content to tolerate Jews, Muslims and pagans, limits to religious toleration were imposed by his view of the contemporary State and society. For example (although his opinion changed throughout his writings on this point), Locke would not extend toleration to Roman Catholics because he saw their adherence to the Pope as being to a human authority to rival the State, nor to atheists, because the inability to swear an oath was, he considered, destructive of social obligations. In short, Locke gives a Christian audience some powerful reasons for toleration that they will easily recognise and accept but does not provide (or aim to provide) a general case for toleration in a Liberal State. A wider focus on biblical principles is necessary to extract principles which will assist with contemporary preoccupations.

This is not the place for a full treatment of the theology of the State [44] nor of Christian perspectives on civil disobedience. [45] Those are important

---

[43] For general accounts of the limitations of Locke's argument see M. Cranston, 'John Locke and the Case for Toleration', and J. Waldron, 'Locke: Toleration and the Rationality of Persecution', in Horton and Mendus, *op. cit.*, n. 40.

[44] For useful historical overviews see: Lyall, *op. cit.*, n. 2, ch. 1 and M.H. Ogilvie, *Religious Institutions and the Law in Canada*, (Toronto, Carswell, 1996), ch. 1. For discussion of models of church-state relations in contem- porary Europe see I.C. Ibán, *op. cit.*, n. 29; S. Ferrari, 'The New Wine and the Old Cask. Tolerance, Religion and the Law in Contemporary Europe', (1997), 10 *Ratio Juris*, 75.

[45] For a helpful discussion in the context of US constitutional history see John W. Whitehead, *Civil Disobedience: A Judeo-Christian Perspective*, (Charlottesville, VA, 1993).

questions whose ramifications extend beyond the boundaries of the present discussion. However, we can sketch one major difference to the Liberal approach. For modern Liberals religious liberty is a limited, subordinate or secondary idea (it exists granted a civil society or consti - tution). Under a Christian perspective, however, it is the State which is subordinate: government is a God-given institution which operates within limits; these limits include the obligation on believers to obey God rather than men if a choice has to be made. Examples in both the Old and New Testaments show divine approval of resistance by believers of attempts by State officials to silence preaching or prevent prayer. The same tradition is reflected in Natural Law theories, from Aquinas to Finnis.

We need to distinguish between the attitudes of Christians as electors and as political agents from those as citizens. The New Testament is quite clear about the Christian perspective on the role as *citizens*. State authority is treated as divinely ordained and therefore Christians are to obey the law and pay taxes since government is a general blessing ordained by God for the benefit of mankind (Rom. 13:1–6; Tit. 3:1). However, if asked to do something directly contrary to God's instruction Christians should refuse: see the example in Acts 4:19 of Peter and John who refused to be silenced when instructed by the authorities because they obeyed God not men (and see also Dan. 3:1–30; 6:7–25 and Acts 12). We can understand the commands of the authorities in such cases to be *ultra vires* (beyond their powers) if they ask obedience of this kind; [46] Jesus said we were to render to Caesar what is Caesar's and to God what is rightfully his. This implies limits to our obedience to the State. We might say that such laws or orders fail to create an obligation to obey, notwithstanding the presumptive force and respect normally given to the law.

Moreover, not every action of a public official is lawful. The behaviour of Paul in Phillipi who invoked his Roman citizenship against the officials (Acts 16:37) supports the Christian's right to insist on his civil liberties when confronted with unlawful demands. At a later point in Acts Paul used his citizenship again to appeal to Caesar with the result that he was taken to Rome for trial (Acts 23:24–29; 28:19). Assertion of legal rights may be one way in which evil people are restrained in positions of power they enjoy and which others (such as those unable to help themselves, e.g., the unborn, the alien, the poor, and the sick) are defended. Christian citizens are entitled within a non-Christian State to use the flawed constitutional protections to hand, [47] although they may not assent to all aspects of their philosophical or political founda - tions. In the same way, at the present time many Christians harbour

---

[46]   Cf. Aquinas, *Summae Theologica*, Q95 A2.

[47]   Christians are not, however, to be litigious (particularly among each other) since this is a poor witness: 1 Cor. 6:1–7.

reservations about international and constitutional statements of human rights, not least because of their individualism and the lack of reciprocal responsibilities within such charters. Nevertheless, this should not be regarded as a fundamental objection to taking advantage of the legal protection which rights such as freedom of religion may offer.

The second aspect – Christian behaviour as electors and political actors – is less clear on historical precedent, since we have no direct biblical parallels. Modern Britain is neither an Old Testament theocracy nor an alien empire in which Christians are merely a persecuted minority and wholly without political power. In a democracy we are, in a sense, in the position of being the ruler as well as the subject. We should therefore aim to love our neighbour as ourselves *through* the political process. Christians will obviously differ on the specifics of a political programme, but there is no room for an attitude of disinterested withdrawal from the political process, since we are in a sense responsible before God for the laws made on our behalf. Christians are therefore fully entitled to use the political and legislative process to do all they can to protect others from harm. However, a Christian approach to what constitutes harm to others will often be contentious within a Liberal society. For example, because we recognise the reality of moral harm such protection may sometimes take the form of paternalism and appear to cut across other values Liberals respect, especially freedom of choice. Furthermore, as a minority within a Liberal society we are as entitled as any other group to ask for laws protecting and respecting our conscientious position when the majority take a different view, which they wish to pursue. Liberals cannot deny such protection without self-contradiction since even if they do not hold a Christian position, they are committed to respecting its integrity.

The public/private divide warrants discussion also. Jesus' injunction to render to God what is God's and to Caesar what is Caesar's (Mt. 22:21) might appear to lend some support for the treatment of religious allegiance as a privatised matter. However, as we have just seen, the behaviour of early Christians and of Jesus himself recorded in the gospel accounts does not support the view that any such public/private divide should be accepted *in the place where the State chooses to draw it*. Moreover, Christians are under a clear duty to manifest their faith, rather than treating it merely as a matter of private belief. The public/private distinction can be made in two different senses: as the boundary marker for individual freedom (including religious freedom) or as the limit of permissible State competence – a matter to be judged by believers.

In the first sense the traditional approach of the common law in England whereby (the Church of England excepted) churches are seen as voluntary, self-governing bodies allows for a measure of religious freedom. Likewise, the existence of a system of ecclesiastical courts suggested a recognition of the boundary, although the jurisdiction originally included many matters to do with family law and succession also. This need not imply exemption from normal legal jurisdiction (for example, in rules applicable to property or trusts) or necessarily require special privileges. (However, in practice religious groups, even outside the established church, have enjoyed various fiscal and other privileges not available to secular bodies.) When churches or related institutions, for example, claim that recognition should be given to their doctrinal beliefs by exemption from general non-discrimination principles over the treatment of women (as regards priesthood) or, perhaps in the not-so-distant future, with regard to practising homosexuals, they are arguing for the respecting of a private sphere in this way. [48] The whole question of legal recognition of tests of membership for faith communities and their right to discipline or expel members likewise raises issues concerning this boundary. To some extent the acceptance of such practices is implicit in the recognition of freedom to associate with others in order to practise one's own religion. [49] However, it brings into sharp focus conflict for the State between individual and collective rights of freedom of religion.

The New Testament contains some principles which assist in handling questions of individual conscience within the church body, notably, the so-called 'weaker brethren' rule which Paul expounds in dealing with the question of food which may have been offered to idols (1 Cor. 10:25–11:1); it is notable that the problem of how to approach food offered to idols concerned how to approach the beliefs and consciences of both non-Christians and Christians alike. However, this principle is not invoked with regard to circumcision – which Paul opposes as detracting from true faith in Galatians (especially Gal. 5:2–6), suggesting that discrimination is required in handling claims allegedly based on conscience. In Matthew we find Jesus paying the temple tax so as not to offend (Mt. 17:24–27).

For Christians, freedom of religion can never be an end in its own right, nor is it a necessary condition for living a Christian life, as a recent survey of the persecution and harassment of an estimated 650 million Christians world-wide shows. [50] Jesus' instructions to the church were not conditional on a favourable democratic climate; the early church thrived in a hostile climate where its religious liberties were routinely denied not just by powerful and favoured religious bodies, but also by local and other State officials, and through societal persecution. Christians have little

---

[48] The principle allowing otherwise indirectly discriminatory conduct to be justified in anti-discrimination law may have the same result; see for example *Bd of Govns of St Matthias C of E Church School* v *Crizzle*, [1993] ICR 401 (requirement of a Christian school for a Headteacher who was a practising Christian in communion held to be justifiable under the Race Relations Act 1976, s. 1(1)(b)(ii)).

[49] Freedom of association is protected under Article 11 of the European Convention on Human Rights.

[50] P. Marshall, *Their Blood Cries Out*, (Word, Texas, 1997).

biblical mandate for asserting an absolute right to a particular form of democratic government and a particular set of freedoms, including freedom of religion. However, freedom of religion is an instrumental good; it allows liberty to evangelise more easily than where it is absent.

Moreover, a respect for freedom of conscience and absence of coercion in belief reflect the Christian understanding of the nature of God and his treatment of human nature. If, as Christians believe, God has given individuals freedom to respond or not to his love, then should not institutions shaped and influenced by Christians respect this same free - dom?[51] Christians will want to campaign for laws which respect and promote this attribute of human dignity. Controversially, this may include respecting freedom of choice with regard to life-altering deci - sions, such as refusal of medical treatment for reasons of conscience or religious belief.[52] Whereas Liberals who regard human freedom of choice as the highest good sometimes justify paternalistic intervention on the pretext of preserving *future* freedom of choice,[53] Christians may wish to affirm that dignity requires recognition of the validity and finality of the choices made whether for good reasons or bad. There is also a self-interested reason: the argument that people making 'irrational' commit - ments and choices should be protected from themselves until they see things differently could too easily be used against Christian belief and action in the future.

Respect for human dignity is, however, a secondary concern for Christians to spreading the gospel itself. An example may help to show why an ordering of principles is necessary: it is easy to imagine circum - stances in which another religious group claims that their freedom of religion has been infringed by public proclamation of Jesus' statement that he is the way, the truth and the life. Freedom of religious expression may in some circumstances run directly counter to freedom not to have deeply held religious and other beliefs disturbed by words and actions

---

[51]   See T. Lorenzen, 'The Theological Basis for Religious Liberty: A Christian Perspective', (1979), *Journal of Church and State*, 415–430.

[52]   Different considerations may arise, however, as regards the refusal of treat-ment by a parent on behalf of a child, or the withdrawal of treatment at the request or with the consent of relatives from a person dependent for continued well-being on intervention by medical staff (whether or not the law would regard this as constituting treatment). Nor should I be taken as condoning suicide or arguing that the law should allow others (whether or not medically qualified) to assist in taking another's life at their request. All of these are distinguishable in my view (albeit, narrowly) from the question of whether refusal of treatment for oneself (where the intervention of no-one else is involved) should be respected.

[53]   See J. Lively, 'Paternalism', in A. P. Griffiths (ed.), *Of Liberty*, (Cambridge, 1983).

considered offensive. The Christian message of universal sin, the unique -
ness of Christ, and his work of atonement and individual salvation is by
nature divisive and offensive to many people. However, a law which
protected people from having cherished ideas disturbed in this way could
not be claimed to allow meaningful freedom of religion of the type which
Christians wish to practice.

Blasphemy

The same point has implications for the existence or scope of a law of
blasphemy. Christians who want the freedom to profess their faith in a
way which others may find offensive ought to feel some inconsistency
in denying the same freedom to other people through retention of the
current offence of blasphemy. Much confusion exists about the rationale
of the blasphemy law, certainly among those who criticise it, but even
among those who argue for its retention or extension to other faiths.

The interest here is not so much in the substantive elements of the
offence but in the types of argument which are deployed in debates about
its scope and operation. Following its resuscitation in 1979 by Mrs Mary
Whitehouse in a private prosecution against the editor of *Gay News*,
Dennis Lemon,[54] blasphemy has enjoyed a fragile existence. No further
prosecutions have succeeded but Muslims angered at the content of
Salman Rushdie's *The Satanic Verses* unsuccessfully attempted to com-
mence proceedings,[55] highlighting in the process the extent to which the
offence is concerned solely with attacks on Christianity.

Although prosecutions are extremely rare[56] the offence probably ex-
ercises more influence collaterally in guiding the editorial decisions of
broadcasters through incorporation in the various codes.[57] In the most
recent example the British Board of Film Classification refused a licence
to a video film depicting the life of St Teresa of Avila; the European
Court of Human Rights found that there had been no violation of Article
10 of the ECHR.[58] This influence can, however, be overstated. It has
not, for example, inhibited the broadcasting of either current affairs and
documentary-style material, such as *Heart of the Matter*, which frequently
airs material hostile to orthodox Christian belief, or serious drama
portraying Christianity or aspects of it in an extremely negative light,
such as Jeanette Winterton's *Oranges are Not the Only Fruit* or Dennis

---

[54] *Whitehouse v Lemon* [1979] AC 617. Note that in Scotland blasphemy no
      longer exists as a distinct offence: Lyall, *op. cit.*, n. 2 at 139.
[55] *R v Chief Metropolitan Magistrate, ex p. Choudhury* [1991] QB 429.
[56] The last two successful prosecutions were brought in 1922 and 1978.
[57] Cf. A. Bradney, *op. cit.*, n. 21 at 97 arguing that blasphemy remains a real if
      qualified constraint on freedom of speech through self-censorship.
[58] *Wingrove v UK, The Times*, Law Report, December 5 1996.

Potter's *Brimstone and Treacle*. Certainly some Christians have responded with demands that the blasphemy laws be invoked, but the fact remains that no prosecutions have been brought and, in view of the high standards of offensiveness of tone (rather than content) required, it is hard to see how they could be. On the other hand, one area of censorship which is seldom noticed or lamented by Liberals is the enforced absence of broadcast evangelism from non-satellite television and radio in Britain. [59] Broadcasters demonstrate their Liberalism by giving regular access to 'excluded' ethnic or sexual minorities, while evangelical Christians, who surely equally qualify for minority status according to the Liberal vision of multi-culturalism, are almost uniquely disfavoured.

Blasphemy poses particular difficulties for would-be law reformers because of ambivalence over which of two Liberal virtues should prevail. The common law offence is routinely attacked for the 'protection' (a term I would avoid, since it begs considerable questions about the rationale of the offence) it gives to Christians (and to Anglicans in particular), which is regarded as discriminatory within a multi-faith society. On this argument pluralism requires equal protection of all religions from attack and protection of the religious feelings of all. [60] However, Liberals are also troubled by the restriction on free speech which blasphemy represents, the logic of which suggests that abolition [61] rather than extension of the offence would be the better course. It can also be argued that abolition of the offence would produce equal treatment of religions in that none would be protected from attack. [62] Although this inconclusive debate has continued for a century at least, both arguments have been revived in recent years in the light of the response of the Muslim community to the publication of Salman Rush - die's book *The Satanic Verses*. [63] For Liberals, blasphemy has come almost to exemplify the problem of intolerance of intolerance.

[59]   See I. Leigh, *op. cit.* n. 36, discussing the Broadcasting Act 1990 and related Codes of Practice.

[60]   As advocated by Lord Scarman in *Whitehouse v Gay News Ltd. and Lemon* [1979] AC 617, 658 (although for Lord Scarman's later views see Unsworth, *op. cit.*, n. 22 at 672–4); this was also the approach of a minority of the Law Commission in the report, *Criminal Law: Offences Against Religion and Public Worship*, Law Com. 145 (1985); Archbishop of Canterbury's Working Group, *Offences Against Religion and Public Worship*, (1988); S. Poulter, 'Towards Legislative Reform of the Blasphemy and Racial Hatred Laws', (1991), *Public Law*, 371.

[61]   As advocated by D.W. Elliott, 'Blasphemy and Other Expressions of Offensive Material', (1993), 11 *Ecclesiastical Law Journal*, 70.

[62]   Bradney, *op. cit.*, n. 21 at 96–7.

[63]   See Bradney, *op. cit.*, n. 21 at 85–91; C. Munro, 'Prophets, Presbyters and Profanity', (1989), *Public Law*, 369 at 369–373.

The continued survival of the offence under modern conditions has been due not just to the ambivalence of reformers and lack of Parliamentary appetite for reform (unsuccessful Private Members' Bills for reform of the offence have been presented for more than a century), but also to what has been described as the 'chameleon-like' capacity of the offence to adapt to changed social conditions.[64] It can be argued credibly that the rationale of the offence has shifted from protection of ideas fundamental to the stability of the State in the seventeenth century,[65] to prevention of public disorder,[66] to prevention of offence to religious feelings.[67] This journey illustrates dramatically changing views of religious belief as Liberalism became ascendant: from belief which grounded the very existence of the State, to in the end belief as essentially a private matter concerned with subjective notions of truth and emotional responses. Although commentators often write as though the offence is a dinosaur from an earlier Christian era, its formulation has since the late nineteenth century been firmly within a Liberal mould, although, admittedly, one not without its contradictions.

The modern scope of the offence is quite restrictive:

> Every publication is said to be blasphemous which contains any contemptu-ous, reviling, scurrilous or ludicrous matter relating to God, Jesus Christ, or the Bible, or the formularies of the Church of England as by law established. It is not blasphemous to speak or publish opinions hostile to the Christian religion, or to deny the existence of God, if the publication is couched in decent and temperate language. The test to be applied is as to the manner in which the doctrines are advocated and not as to the substance of the doctrines themselves.[68]

Vague claims that blasphemy criminalises unbelief or criticism of Christi-anity *per se* or whatever offends individual Christians are, therefore, fanciful, as the European Court of Human Rights has recently recognised.[69]

---

[64]   Munro, *op. cit.*, n. 63 at 371; I. Leigh, 'Not to Judge but to Save?: The Development of the Law of Blasphemy' (1977), *Cambrian Law Review*, 56.

[65]   See *Taylor's Case*, (1696), 1 Ven. 293.

[66]   *Bowman* v *Secular Society Ltd*, [1917] A.C.406, 446 per Lord Parker.

[67]   *Whitehouse* v *Gay News Ltd. and Lemon*, [1979] AC 617; *R* v *Chief Metropolitan Magistrate, ex p. Choudhury* [1991] QB 429.

[68]   *Stephen's Digest of the Criminal Law*, (9th ed., 1950), Art. 214 cited with approval by Lord Scarman in *Whitehouse* v *Gay News Ltd. and Lemon*, [1979] AC 617, 665.

[69]   *Wingrove* v *UK*, (Case 19/1995/525/611) European Court of Human Rights, 25 November 1996, para. 60: 'The extent of insult to religious feelings must be significant as is clear from the use by the courts of the adjectives "contemptuous, reviling, scurrilous or ludicrous" to depict mate-rial of a sufficient degree of offensiveness. The high degree of profanation that must be attained constitutes in itself safeguard against arbitrariness.'

The debate about the future of blasphemy is often marked by an alarmingly ahistorical approach which runs together statements of the rationale of the offence from different eras and treats them as equally valid, invalid or adaptable in contemporary circumstances, depending on the author's position. In the case of justifications long since discarded this allows some spectacular (if hollow) argumentative victories. For example, the notion that protection of Christianity through the criminalisation of those who attack it is central to the continuation of civil society, [70] is an easy target, but that is hardly surprising in view of the fact that this justification for the offence was abandoned by the judges more than a century ago.

However, the same argument looks equally strange dressed as a modern justification for blasphemy – Tregilgas-Davey argues that the dictum of Ashurst J. in Thomas Paine's case from 1797 that 'all offences of this kind are punishable as such, in as much as they weaken those obligations whereby civil society is bound together' can be adapted to provide a justification either for the abolition of blasphemy or its extension to non-Christian religions.

> [E]xtending (or abolishing) the blasphemy laws would not be undermining Christianity, rather it would be a public welcoming to the multi-faith, multi-racial society in which we live, and as such it would be a formal acceptance of all our citizens, no matter what their religion. The existence of a blasphemy law which protects one sect forbids this, thus far from having a cohesive effect on society as the Divisional Court claimed, it prevents the cohesion of our plural society.[71]

The argument is an intriguing one, but it faces a number of difficulties which can be mentioned only in passing. First, even assuming (no evidence of the degree of diversity is offered) that Britain is now as religiously diverse as Tregilgas-Davey asserts, it is for discussion what the role of law ought to be, and what effect it will have in practice. The idea that the law can be a source of social cohesion in a diverse society is

---

[70] For example, Unsworth: '[T]his affinity with sedition underlines the function of the law of blasphemy in securing a politico-religious governmental order, an institutional and symbolic church–state unity which is still of fundamental importance in investing the state with a transcendent and, therefore to its critics, mystificatory form of moral authority in its dealings with transgression' *op. cit.*, n. 22 at 664. While one could plausibly argue that the monarchy plays such a role, to claim that blasphemy does so seems like legal fetishism of a high order. Equally overblown is the same author's conclusion that 'blasphemy will present one of the most decisive indicators of the future cultural direction of the British state' (*ibid.*, 677).

[71] M. Tregilgas-Davey, 'Ex parte Choudhury – An Opportunity Missed', (1991), 51 *Modern Law Review*, 294, 296.

problematic (see the earlier discussion of neutrality), but even accepting that, it is arguable that one of the options on offer (extension of the offence) might undermine rather than buttress social cohesion if it resulted in an increase of prosecutions and a tendency to juridify religious controversy among and between different faiths. Similarly, the argument that the current position undermines social cohesion suggests that blas - phemy is regarded with a symbolic importance greatly exceeding its practical significance in terms of frequency of prosecutions or (I would argue) its inhibition of free speech. Both the timing and context of Ashurst J.'s comment suggest that he would have understood something entirely different by a reference to 'the bonds of civil society'. Writing in 1797 he would have been understood to be invoking a species (probably Lockeian) of social contract theory and the obligations in question were those between the individual and State respectively. Bearing in mind that the target was Thomas Paine's *The Rights of Man*, with its emphasis on government limited by popular sovereignty and individual rights, this is understandable. The connections between religion and the system of government were made not just by the judges repressing expressions of opinion but also by writers such as Paine. None of this transfers easily to a modern Liberal context in which it is tolerance and equality *between individuals* which is assumed to be foundational.

Julian Rivers argues the case for retention of an offence of blasphemy as a symbol of the extent to which current legal values (not least those of tolerance and due process) are dependent on Christian foundations. [72] He would couple this with a broader new offence of incitement to religious hatred applicable to all religions, whose purpose would be to protect believers' feelings and requiring threatening, abusive or insulting words or behaviour used with intent to outrage, or likelihood of outraging, the feelings of a significant number of a recognised religious group. The inter-relationship between the new offence and the old might be more problematic than Rivers allows. The difficulty is that the new offence would be simultaneously wider (not just with regard to religions covered, but also because of a weaker standard of reaction in the putative 'victim') and narrower (because of the requirement of intention to outrage religious feelings) [73] than the common law offence of blasphemy. How - ever, if the reform worked as intended and the common law remained in somnolence, it would do little to abate the criticism of those, like Tregilgas-Davey, whose main objection is not just that other religious groups' feelings go unprotected, but also that it is offensive to accord a privileged position to Christianity.

[72]   A.J. Rivers, *Blasphemy in the Secular State*, (*Cambridge Papers*, Vol. 1, No. 4, 1992).

[73]   The *Gay News* decision confirms that the only *mens rea* requirement for blasphemy is an intention to *publish*.

The difficulty blasphemy poses by way of clashing of freedom of speech and freedom of religion has been highlighted by recent cases under the European Convention on Human Rights. In three cases the Convention's organs have attempted to resolve any apparent conflict between Articles 9 and 10 of the Convention, in finding that restrictions on freedom of expression can be permissible when their purpose is to protect religious feelings from vilification. In the 1994 *Otto-Preminger Institute* case the European Court of Human Rights held the seizure and forfeiture of a satirical antireligious film (*Das Liebenkonsil*) in the Tyrol did not contravene Article 10, since its purpose was the protection of the rights of others (those rights themselves recognised under Article 9 as well as in the exceptions to Article 10).[74] Similar reasoning was followed in the recent *Wingrove* case from the UK when the European Court of Human Rights found that the decision of the Video Appeals Committee upholding the refusal of the British Board of Film Classification to grant a certificate for the video *Visions of Ecstasy*, on the grounds that it could be considered blasphemous, did not violate Article 10.[75] However, the Court laid less emphasis on Article 9 than in its earlier ruling. Pointing to the continued survival of blasphemy legislation in various European countries, the Court invoked the margin of appreciation doctrine:

> . . . there is no uniform European conception of the requirements of the protection of the rights of others in relation to attacks on their religious convictions. What is likely to cause substantial offence to persons of a particular religious persuasion will vary significantly from time to time and place to place, especially in an era characterised by an ever growing array of faiths and denominations. By reason of their direct and continuous contact with the vital forces of their countries, State authorities are in a better position than the international judge to give an opinion on the exact content of these requirements with regard to the rights of others as well as the necessity of a restriction intended to protect from such material those whose deepest feelings and convictions would be seriously offended.[76]

In *Wingrove* the European Court of Human Rights declined to rule on whether because the law of blasphemy treated attacks on Christianity differently to other religions, this amounted to a violation of the Conven -tion. When *Choudhury* reached the Commission it held that a failure to criminalise publications offending non-Christians did not of itself amount to a violation of freedom of religion and that since there was no right to

---

[74] *Otto-Preminger Institute* v *Austria*, Series A 295, (1994).
[75] *Wingrove* v *UK*, *op. cit.*, n. 69. Earlier the Commission had held that the *Gay News* prosecution did not raise an admissible claim to a violation of the Convention: *X Ltd. and Y* v *UK*, No. 8710/ 79, 28 Decisions and Reports (DR) 77, (1982); sub. nom. *Gay News* v *UK*, (1983), 5 EHRR, 123.
[76] *Wingrove*, *op. cit.*, n. 69, para. 58.

be protected in this way no question concerning discrimination in the enjoyment of a Convention right for the purpose of Article 14 arose. [77] It is clear, therefore, that despite the reasoning that blasphemy offences can be justified under Article 10, if the offence were abolished there would be no violation of Article 9 from the failure by the State to protect against offensive speech. The result may appear paradoxical but any contradiction is subsumed under the margin of appreciation which the Convention organs allow to national authorities. A leading textbook on the Convention argues that the Court of Human Rights should follow the logic of the strong statements in favour of positive protection of freedom of religion in the *Otto-Preminger* case and require the State to grant protection against peaceful enjoyment of their religious beliefs to minorities also. [78]

However, any development along these lines would inevitably raise the spectre of blasphemy law becoming the locus of religious controversy, with opposing groups claiming a right to be protected against offence from the mere expression or manifestation of the other's beliefs. At present the law avoids such conflict not just by its partial coverage but also by the high degree of offensiveness required in the manner of the speech. Significantly, one commentator has suggested that any attempt to extend the blasphemy laws to other religions would also have to take account of differing thresholds of offence, impliedly lowering the standard in the case of Muslims, or the 'protection' offered would be illusory. [79] Although Unsworth passes this off with a postmodern flourish ('the question of how the law is to negotiate the phenomenon of difference in the contempo - rary'), the contradiction ought to trouble Liberals, quite apart from whether it could be reconciled with Article 14 of the Convention. With the incorporation of the European Convention into United Kingdom law in the Human Rights Act, and without the shield of the margin of appreciation to shelter behind, English judges may soon find the issue of the coverage of blasphemy presenting itself for reconsideration. It is plain that following the lines advocated by Lord Scarman in the *Gay News* case and extending the scope of the offence could cause considerable difficulties.

Christians have special reason to be sceptical about blasphemy also, even though they are its ostensible beneficiaries. The foremost is that Jesus himself was condemned for the equivalent offence [80] by the Jewish rulers of the day (Mt. 26:65–66; Mk. 14:64). Stephen, the first Christian martyr, was stoned on the basis of the same charge (Acts 6:11–7:60). Secondly, while the New Testament certainly suggests a variety of responses towards heresy *within the church*, these all leave ultimate punishment in the hands of God (cf. the parable of the weeds: Mt. 13:24–30, especially v. 30).

---

[77]   *Choudhury* v *UK*, No. 17439/90, 12 HRLJ (1991).

[78]   D. Harris, M. O'Boyle, and C. Warbrick, *Law of the European Convention on Human Rights*, (London, 1995), 359–360 and 362.

[79]   Unsworth, *op. cit.*, n. 22 at 676–7.

[80]   For the Old Testament basis see: Lev. 24:10–16; Exod. 20:7; Deut. 13.

Punishment of blasphemy cannot, of course, literally *protect* Christ or his reputation, an objective which is either presumptuous or futile. When people claim to be doing so they are best understood as expressing the strong nature of the offence which *they* have suffered. Attractive as recognition of religious sensitivity may be as a way of expressing freedom of religion, the history of the early church gives little warrant for contem - porary Christians to assume that they have a right to be protected from offence or abuse in this way. Exposure to offensive *speech* or *images* falls a long way short of the persecution suffered by the early Christians, or the beatings, torture, rape, murder and institutionalised slavery and discrimination which millions of Christians face around the world today.

To be absolutely truthful, most of the offence caused by instances in which British Christians have argued for the invocation of blasphemy in recent decades has been in a sense artificially manufactured – the offence is at the *idea* that certain words or images have been created. Few Christians, for example, would have read for themselves or been offended by James Kirkup's poem published in *Gay News*, which gave rise to the Lemon prosecution. In reality, the prosecution almost certainly gave the poem itself a wider circulation than it would otherwise have enjoyed, gave wide publicity through the media to the ideas which were offensive, and in the longer term considerably aided the cause of homosexual rights in Britain by martyring the paper's editor in the eyes of Liberals. Although no prosecutions were brought, it seems equally likely that the controversy surrounding the films *The Life of Brian* and *The Last Temptation of Christ* were a gift to the grateful distributors and recipients of royalties cheques. This is not to argue that attacks on the character of Jesus should be stoically tolerated; on the contrary, they should be opposed by every argument and at every opportunity in the name of truth, and scholarly and historical accuracy (controversy of this kind is often an evangelistic opportunity in its own right as Paul himself recognised). But to criminalise those who make them helps neither the individuals concerned nor society in general. Rather than extending the offence of blasphemy, it should now be abolished; doing so would have the incidental advantage of removing the misleading argument that the law concerning freedom of expression somehow grants special privileges to Christians.

Freedom of religion and a Bill of Rights in the UK[81]

If blasphemy is one case study of the conflict in the Liberal and Christian approaches, the current debate over incorporation of the European

---

[81] The literature is voluminous, but for treatments from specifically Christian perspectives see: R. Song, *Christianity and Liberal Society*, (Oxford, 1997), ch. 6 (dealing with constitutional review) and J. Rivers, 'A Bill of Rights for the United Kingdom?', in P. Beaumont (ed.), *Christian Perspectives on Law Reform*, (Carlisle, 1998), 25–50.

Convention on Human Rights (ECHR) is a second. Much of the debate over the last quarter of a century in the UK about a domestic Bill of Rights has focused on the need for such a change, the status of the document, and its effect on the judiciary, rather than on its contents. On the model of the ECHR it has been assumed by many commentators that freedom of religion should feature, but few have given much discussion to the content of the right.

The European Convention on Human Rights contains the following:

Article 9:
1. Everyone has the right to freedom of thought, conscience and religion; this right includes freedom to change his religion or belief and freedom, either alone or in community with others or in public or private, to manifest his religion or belief, in worship, teaching, practice and observance.
2. Freedom to manifest one's religion or beliefs shall be subject only to such limitations as are prescribed by law and are necessary in a democratic society in the interest of public safety, for protection of public order, health or morals, or for the protection of the rights and the freedoms of others.[82]

Article 14:
The enjoyment of the rights and freedoms set forth in this Convention shall be secured without discrimination on any grounds such as sex, race, colour, language, religion, political or other opinion, national or social origin, association with a national minority, property, birth or other status.

An alternative approach is Liberty's document of 1991 *A People's Charter* which follows closely Article 9 of the ECHR, except that freedom of thought, conscience and religion is expressly stated to include the right for everyone 'to hold their own opinions' and 'the right to no religion' and the permissible restrictions on manifesting one's religion would be significantly narrower and available only where:

. . . prescribed by law, strictly necessary and demonstrably justified in a democratic society for the protection of individuals from imminent physical harm and for the protection of rights and freedom of others as laid down in this Bill.

Liberty cites as examples of how such restrictions might be relevant the refusal to ordain women and refusal of life-saving medical treatment as regards a child for religious reasons.[83] The wider restrictions permitted under Article 9 (for example, on grounds of public health) would therefore be impermissible.

[82]   On the scope of Article 9 see D. Harris, M. O'Boyle and C. Warbrick, *The Law of the European Convention on Human Rights*, (London, 1995), ch. 10; P.W. Edge, *op. cit.*, n. 30 above; H. Cullen, 'The Emerging Scope of Freedom of Conscience', (1997), 22 *European Law Review*, HRC / 32; M. Evans, *Religious Liberty and International Law in Europe*, (Cambridge, 1997).

[83]   Liberty, *A People's Charter*, (London, 1991), 58–9.

Prior to its election as the new government in 1997, Labour had pledged itself to incorporate the ECHR into domestic law as a prelude to the more fundamental change of introducing a home-grown Bill of Rights. [84] Following the election a White Paper[85] on incorporation of the Convention and a Human Rights Bill were published in October 1997. At the time of writing the Bill is in the Commons' Committee stage, and some important amendments to the original proposals affecting freedom of religion have been made as a response to earlier changes during the House of Lords debates. The Bill will oblige UK courts to interpret legislation where possible consistently with the Convention rights, including Article 9 and, in so doing, to take account of the case law from the European Commission and Court of Human Rights; where UK legislation is incompatible courts from the High Court and Court of Session up may give a declaration of incompatibility, but they will have no power to set the offending legislation aside. The Labour Government is committed to giving the superior courts in Scotland the power to set aside legislation of the Scottish Parliament which is incompatible with the European Convention on Human Rights. A 'fast track' procedure for amending UK law in conformity with the Convention is introduced by the Human Rights Bill, triggered either by a declaration of incompatibility or by rulings from the Strasbourg court (whether or not in a case involving the UK). This procedure is controver - sial because of the discretion which it will give to the Executive in implementing changes to the law in compliance with the Convention at the expense of normal legislative processes.

However, a number of aspects of the possible impact of the Bill are conjectural. The main area of uncertainty concerns possible 'horizontal effect' of the Bill as between private individuals, rather than between individuals and governmental agencies. Uncertainty has arisen because of the inclusion in the Bill of somewhat tortuous drafting making a court a public authority which is bound to act consistently with a person's Convention rights (unless required clearly to override them by legisla - tion).[86] Although this could be regarded as requiring the court to apply the substance of the law to achieve compatibility with the Convention wherever possible (and not just with regard to legislation), if necessary by overturning settled common law rules, the better interpretation is that it is intended to import the Convention standards into court procedures and discretionary decisions (for example, the scope of remedies awarded). [87]

---

[84] Labour Party, *Bringing Rights Home*, (London, 1996).

[85] *Rights Brought Home*, (Cm. 3782, 1997).

[86] Cl. 6(3).

[87] This view is consistent both with the White Paper and the Lord Chancellor's statements (see n. 88 and 89 below) and with the structure of the Bill itself. If 'full' horizontal effect were intended the Bill might have been expected to contain a general clause equivalent to the interpretive duty imposed in relation to legislation (cl. 3(1)).

The discussion of possible horizontal effect is significant in the case of freedom of religion as regards possible remedies for religious discrimination, or apparent sex or race discrimination where a purported justification of freedom of conscience or religion is claimed, and as regards possible enforcement of discriminatory covenants, trusts and testamentary gifts. Moreover, internal procedures for church discipline could run the risk of a clash between Articles 9 and 10 (freedom of speech) or Article 8 (respect for privacy, which has been interpreted to require recognition of sexual autonomy) if horizontal effect applies.

Lack of space precludes a full discussion of possible horizontal effect. However, a few comments can be made pertinent to freedom of religion. First, the government did not intend that the Human Rights Bill would be a source of new legal rights and obligations between individuals and unlike, for example, the 1996 South African Constitution, it contains no statement that it applies to individuals. To that extent private law should not be affected. The Lord Chancellor specifically stated during the Second Reading debate on the Bill in the House of Lords that it was not intended to apply between private individuals, [88] although in a later debate he indicated that the courts would be able (as under the existing law) to refer to the Convention as a source of inspiration in developing the common law principles applicable between private individuals. [89] One eminent public lawyer has argued that this is an inconsistent and unclear position, [90] but it is similar to that adopted in other countries which have adopted domestic human rights protections, notably Canada. [91] It is probably more helpful to distinguish between differing degrees of horizontal effect: if the Bill is not intended to have 'full' horizontal effect, nevertheless it may be relevant as between private individuals in a diluted form as a background consideration. Some of the previous occasions where the courts have looked to the ECHR as a source of inspiration in the development of the common law have been exclusively of a private law type (for example, in considering public policy as a reason for not giving effect to the forfeiture of a gift in a will should the beneficiary be or become a Roman Catholic). [92]

---

[88]   HL Debs., 3 November 1997, col. 1231.

[89]   HL Debs., 24 November 1997, col. 783.

[90]   Sir William Wade, 'The United Kingdom's Bill of Rights', in The University of Cambridge Centre for Public Law, *Constitutional Reform in the United Kingdom: Practices and Principles*, (Oxford, 1998), 62–64.

[91]   *Retail Wholesale and Department Store Union Local 580 et al.* v *Dolphin Delivery Ltd.*, (1985), 33 Dominion Law Reports (DLR) (4th) 174. See the helpful analysis in G.W. Anderson, 'The Limits of Constitutional Law: The Canadian Charter of Rights and Freedoms and the Public–Private Divide', in C. Gearty and A. Tomkins (eds.), *Understanding Human Rights*, (London, 1996).

[92]   *Blaythwayt* v *Baron Cawley*, [1976] AC 397; however, in this instance the House of Lords declined to strike down the forfeiture clause.

Another situation where horizontal effect will apply is if the relation - ship between the private parties is founded on legislation: here the courts would be bound as far as possible to interpret it consistent with the parties' Convention rights,[93] including Articles 9 and 14, prohibiting discrimina - tion in the enjoyment of Convention rights, *inter alia*, on grounds of religion. This could arise as a live issue concerning the scope of anti-discrimination legislation, because Northern Ireland aside (where the Fair Employment (Northern Ireland) Act 1989 prohibits some forms of discrimination), religious discrimination is generally not unlawful in the UK. The Commission for Racial Equality has called for the introduction of general legislation against religious discrimination[94] but, hitherto, religious minorities have had to rely instead on a convergence of religious adherence and other factors in order to claim the status of a 'racial group' in the event of indirect racial discrimination.[95] Moreover, religious liberty may also be argued by way of defence to allegedly indirectly discrimina - tory action: incorporation of Article 9 would therefore also become relevant to the question of justification.

Also significant is the new duty imposed on public authorities under clause 6 of the Human Rights Bill to respect a person's Convention rights.[96] Where more detailed and clear primary legislation applies this may have little impact: for example, legislation on religious matters affecting State schools[97] is detailed and leaves little scope for interpolation using Convention rights. However, problems could arise over public

---

[93] This is the effect of cl. 3(1) of the Human Rights Bill.

[94] Commission for Racial Equality, *Second Review of the Race Relations Act*, (London, 1992). See also the Religious Discrimination Bill 1998.

[95] *Mandla* v *Dowell Lee*, [1983] 2 AC 548, holding that Sikhs constitute a 'racial group'; cf. *Seide* v *Gillette Industries*, [1980] Industrial Relations Law Reports (IRLR), 427 as regards Jews; Rastafarians have been held not to be a 'racial group' in *Crown Suppliers* v *Dawkins*, [1991] IRLR 327. Muslims have been held not to constitute an ethnic group but rather an (unprotected) religious one: *JH Walker* v *Hussain*, [1996] IRLR 11; see Bradney, *op. cit.*, n. 21 at 111–2 and S. Poulter, 'Muslim Headscarves in School: Contrasting Legal Approaches in England and France', (1997), 17 *Oxford Journal of Legal Studies*, 43 at 64–5.

[96] Cl. 6(1), 'It is unlawful for a public authority to act in a way which is incompatible with one or more of the Convention rights.'

[97] In England and Wales the matter is governed by the Education Act 1996. As regards school worship: requirement for school collective worship wholly or mainly of a broadly Christian character taking the school term as a whole (Education Act 1996, s. 386) subject to a right to withdraw individual children (EA 1996, s. 389) and to school concessions from the Standing Advisory Council on Religious Education (SACRE) to conduct worship distinctive of any faith for all or any of its pupils (but not of any particular Christian or other denomination): EA 1996, ss. 387 and 394.

sector employees' religious convictions. Legislation providing for consci-entious protection for employees in the cases of abortion, human fertil-isation and embryology, and Sunday Trading[98] once again is fairly detailed, but outside these fields there could be more scope for Article 9 to bite via the clause 6 duty. Suppose the situation in *Ahmed* v *ILEA*[99] (in which the Court of Appeal held that a Muslim teacher was not entitled to time off work to attend a mosque) were to recur following incorpo-ration; there would be an argument for saying that the council was acting unlawfully and that the protection against discrimination in the Education Act should be interpreted more generously in the employee's favour (although his later failure under the Convention machinery[100] shows that success would not be guaranteed).

The boundaries of what constitutes a 'public authority' for the purpose of clause 6 are unclear.[101] The House of Lords debates saw several

[97] *(continued)* Regarding religious education: under EA 1996, s. 375, sylla-buses for religious education 'shall reflect the fact the religious traditions in Great Britain are in the main Christian whilst taking account of the teaching and practices of the other principal religions represented in Great Britain'. Parental right of withdrawal from RE (EA 1996, s. 389); provision of alternative instruction according to tenets of parents' religious denomination at no cost to the local education authority (EA 1996, s. 376).

No religious discrimination in hiring staff except in the case of church schools (EA 1996, s.146 and ss. 304–5).

In Scotland the matter is governed by the Education (Scotland) Act 1980, ss. 8–10. Section 8 provides that religious observance and instruction has been the custom in the public schools in Scotland and that this can be discontinued only if the local education authority votes to do so and this resolution is approved by a majority of electors voting in a poll of the local government electors for the educational area. Nothing is stated in the Act about the nature of religious instruction or observance which is offered unless it is a denominational school (most of these are Roman Catholic), see sections. 21, 22C and 22D.

Section 9 gives parents the right to withdraw their children from religious instruction and/or observance. Other safeguards for those wishing to observe their religious beliefs are provided by section 10.

[98] Respectively: Abortion Act 1967, s.4; Human Fertilisation and Embryology Act 1990, s. 38; Sunday Trading Act 1994, s.4 and sched. 4.

[99] [1978] 1 All ER 574.

[100] Declared inadmissible; *Ahmed* v *UK* (1982), 4 EHRR 126. Tribunal cases involving time off work for religious purposes have succeeded, however, under the Race Relations Act 1976: S. Bailey, D. Harris and B. Jones, *Civil Liberties: Cases and Materials*, (4th ed., London, 1995), 606 and 608.

[101] Cl. 6 (3) 'In this section, "public authority" includes . . . (c) any person certain of whose functions are functions of a public nature . . .' '(5) In relation to a particular act, a person is not a public authority by virtue only of subsection (3)(c) if the nature of the act is private.'

unsuccessful attempts to amend the Bill specifically to exclude churches, religious charities and church schools altogether from clause 6, because of concern over possible claims, for example, by those not sharing the same beliefs or by practising homosexuals.[102] Would a church be required to ordain or admit to membership people unable to subscribe to its doctrinal positions or whose lifestyle or morality it regarded as inconsistent with its beliefs? Concerns were expressed that religious charities such as hospices might be forced to employ pro-euthanasia staff. In response the Lord Chancellor went out of his way not to rule out the possibility that a church, religious charity or church school might be a 'public authority', preferring to leave the question to the courts.[103] In the Commons, however, the Home Secretary sought to reassure, arguing that most functions under - taken by churches would be private in nature under clause 6, but that where the church stood in place of the State (for example, in education) it was right that the Convention should apply.[104] In addition to *Hansard*, the courts may turn for guidance on these difficult questions to analogous cases arising in judicial review and under the Convention itself.

As regards judicial review, religious bodies and officials have generally not been treated as exercising public functions. Thus, the position of the Chief Rabbi as the highest source of spiritual guidance to a Jewish congregation has been held not to be subject to judicial review in a case in which he accepted the report of a commission of inquiry into the misconduct of a rabbi, who was then dismissed.[105] Simon Brown J. argued that the Chief Rabbi's functions were intimate, spiritual and religious in character: in the absence of such a role Parliament would not legislate for these functions, nor would the government seek to discharge them. Interestingly (and of potential importance with regard to the Church of England and the Church of Scotland) he argued that the mere recognition of the Chief Rabbi in legislation and the conferral on him of certain statutory powers did not render his other, non-statutory, roles subject to judicial review. Similarly, in a second case the refusal of an Imam (the spiritual leader of a mosque) to admit certain people onto the roll of voters at the mosque was held not to be subject to judicial review.[106] The court found that the case did not have a public law element since it concerned only a small religious community in Luton, there was no statutory underpinning for the Imam's functions and this was not an area in which

---

[102] HL Debs., 24 November 1997, cols. 789ff.

[103] HL Debs., 24 November 1997, cols. 796–7 and 800.

[104] HC Debs., 20 May 1998, col. 1015: '. . . the regulation of divine worship, the administration of the sacrament, admission to church membership or to the priesthood and decisions of parochial church councils about the running of the parish church are, in our judgment, all private matters'.

[105] *R v Chief Rabbi of the United Congregations of Great Britain and the Commonwealth, ex p. Watchmann*, [1993] 2 All ER 249.

[106] *R v Imam of Bury Park Lane Jame Masji Luton, ex p. Sulaiman Ali*, [1992] Crown Office Digest (C.O.D.), 132.

Parliament would intervene if the internal affairs of the mosque were not properly regulated. Moreover, the court felt incompetent to undertake an examination of religious law and customs and the traditions of the local religious community which would be fundamental to determining the issue.[107]

So far as the status of churches under the Convention is concerned, recognition of freedom of belief under Article 9, freedom of association under Article 11 and of non-discrimination on grounds of religion or belief under Article 14 necessarily implies that churches are to be treated as private and largely self-regulating bodies. The Convention organs have, therefore, refused to intervene in a doctrinal dispute over the form of liturgy to be used.[108] In this (admissibility) decision the Commission reasoning was that the church in question (the Church of Sweden) was a non-governmental organisation, despite being established under public law, because it did not exercise governmental powers and therefore the State was not responsible for its actions.

A variety of tests of the degree of connection between a religious body and the State might be devised to determine whether it is a public authority for the purpose of the Human Rights Bill. Firstly, one might assess exclusivity and legal privilege enjoyed by the church.[109] Secondly, whether the church acts as a State substitute – that is fulfilling functions which the State would undertake if the church did not function. Thirdly, regard might be had to the degree of legal underpinning and State support of the church's activities. Alternatively, consideration might be given to the degree of practical autonomy which the church enjoys.[110] These tests might well produce differing results, depending on the church and the activity in question. The first and third tests might tend to point in general

---

[107] Similar reasoning was used to justify not assuming jurisdiction with regard to a supposed error of law by a Church of England Consistory Court in *R v Chancellor of St Edmundsbury and Ipswich Diocese, ex p. White* , [1948], 1 KB 195.

[108] *Finska Församlingen i Stockholm v Sweden*, App. 24019/94 (1996), 85-A DR 94. Even if this hurdle was overcome, the freedom of the individual to leave a religious group with whom he or she is in dispute and to join another or form one with different beliefs is also a reason for not holding there to be a violation of Article 9: *Karlsson v Sweden*, App. No. 12356/ 86, 57 DR 172 (1988).

[109] The existence of a church established under national law has been held not to violate the Convention *per se*: *Darby v Sweden*, (1991), 13 EHRR 774.

[110] A somewhat similar test has been used in Canada to determine which public institutions are governmental bodies for the purpose of being bound by the Charter of Rights. A university and a hospital have been held to be sufficiently autonomous to be immune from Charter scrutiny despite being in receipt of government funding: *McKinney v University of Guelph*, (1990), 76 DLR (4th) 545; *Stoffman v Vancouver General Hospital*, (1990), 76 DLR (4th) 700, respectively.

towards the view that in England the Church of England is a public authority, although if it did not exist one cannot imagine legislators feeling the need to create it. Liability under the Human Rights Act might be seen as the legal price of the privileges of the establishment – the position of the monarch and of the bishops in the House of Lords are often regarded as Anglican privileges (although to many within the Church of England they are a frequent source of embarrassment in practice). Church schools might likewise be regarded as public authorities. [111] They maintain a distinctive religious ethos under the terms of their trust deeds, but are also in many cases underpinned by a specific statutory regime designed to secure their special position outside local education authority control but within the State framework for most purposes. Most of their funding comes from the State. They have, therefore, according to the third test, legislative and financial underpinning for their activities and, according to the fourth criterion, only relative autonomy.

Even if in applying some such test a church were to be found to be a public authority it would also be necessary to consider the nature of the activity in question, which, if it is intrinsically private, would not attract Human Rights Act protection. Further complexities arise here; is a marriage ceremony to be treated as a private matter and is it relevant whether the ceremony is legally effectual (as in the case of the Church of England)? Should discipline of clergy and issues about ordination be treated as private law questions analogous to employment matters? It would seem anomalous if the result were reached on the basis of the legal parentage of the sources (derived from legislation or delegated legislation) that these questions were subject to the Human Rights Act in the Church of England but not in other denominations. However, it may be the price that has to be paid for the present form of the establishment.

An attempt to exclude churches from the definition of a 'public authority' failed in the House of Lords. Three more limited exemptions met with short-lived success: they were passed only to be removed by the government at the Commons' Committee Stage.

The first was a general defence under the Act for actions 'in pursuance of a manifestation [112] of religious belief in accordance with the historic

---

[111] These are predominantly Church of England and Roman Catholic schools, although a small number of State-supported Jewish schools exist and permission has recently been given for two Muslim schools to be given State funding. In *National Union of Teachers and Others* v *Governing Body of St Mary's Church of England Junior School*, [1997], 3 Common Market Law Reports (CMLR), 630 the English Court of Appeal decided that a Church of England school was an emanation of the State and therefore bound by the vertical direct effect of a European Community Directive.

[112] Inserted as clause 2 (4)–(7). To include 'action such as worship, observance, conformity to moral or ethical principle, practice, teaching and employment policies'.

teaching and practices of a Christian or other principal religious tradition represented in Great Britain'; teaching or practices contravening the criminal law were not covered. The provision would have drawn a court into determining the genuineness of the teaching and whether the practice was 'in accordance with a relevant historic creed, canon, confession of faith, catechism or formulary'. Although apparently very wide, the provision would only have applied *defensively* and to the extent that the Act was interpreted to have horizontal effect or churches were determined to be public authorities for the purpose of clause 6 or where individuals had statutory duties to others. It would have had the effect of giving priority to freedom of religion over other rights, although the clause departed from the pattern of Article 9 for this purpose – only certain beliefs were protected and their manifestations were not subject to justifiable exceptions. The government feared that for this reason the provision might itself be found to violate Articles 9 and 14 and argued also that it was undesirable for secular courts to be involved in determining doctrinal questions.

A second group of amendments was passed to give declaratory effect to earlier ministerial assurances about the scope of the Bill. [113] These were a declaration of the right of 'any minister, official or other person acting on behalf of a Christian or other principal religious tradition represented in Great Britain' not to be compelled under the Act to 'administer a marriage contrary to his religious doctrines or convictions'. [114] Similar amendments were included to allow church schools and religious charities to be able to appoint or dispense with senior staff having regard to whether their 'beliefs and manner of life' are consistent with the 'basic ethos' of the school or charity, respectively. [115] Although these were all deleted in the Commons, the government promised a separate amendment to the Schools Standards and Framework Bill 1998 to meet concerns over appointments to church schools.

Church courts were the object of a specific exemption from the definition of a public authority in clause 6 when exercising, or for acts done within, a jurisdiction 'recognised but not created by Parliament' in

---

[113] HL Debs., 19 January 1998, cols. 1344 and 1346; inserted as cl. 7 (8)–(10).

[114] The Lord Chancellor argued that the exemption was unnecessary to meet concerns about any future hypothetical legal recognition of same-sex contracts because marriage is defined both in domestic law (as to which see Matrimonial Causes Act 1973, s. 11 and Marriage (Scotland) Act 1977, s. 5) and in interpretations of the right to marry under Art. 12 of the ECHR as being between persons of the opposite biological sex. Moreover, concerns that clergy might be compelled to remarry divorcees were equally misplaced since Art. 12 did not confer a right to marry according to a particular form of ceremony and in the case of the Church of England and the Church of Wales (the only churches with a legal obligation to conduct marriages) there is a specific exemption covering the point in legislation: Matrimonial Causes Act 1965, s. 8; see further HL Debs., 5 February 1998, cols. 757–8.

[115] HL Debs., 5 February 1998, cols. 812–3.

matters spiritual.[116] This was intended to exempt the Church of Scotland's kirk session and similar courts of nonconformist churches. The issue reflected wider concerns of the Church of Scotland that the Human Rights Bill represented a break with the settlement arrived at under the 1921 Act where Parliament recognised the exclusive competence of the Church in matters of doctrine, government, worship and discipline.[117] The amendment was deleted in the Commons: the government argued that it was unnecessary and that their new clause (see below) which recognised explicitly that a church was collectively entitled to the benefit of Article 9 would meet any legitimate fears.

The government argued that for the most part the amendments were unnecessary since the concerns were either adequately addressed through the incorporation of Article 9 or under the existing Convention jurispru - dence or subject to specific UK legislative safeguards which would take precedence in the event of conflict, since the Act would only enjoy interpretative status. These reassurances undervalued the extent to which the Bill will allow UK judges to develop a distinctive domestic interpre - tation of the scope of the Convention rights[118] and of the balance between them. Moreover, campaigners were concerned that clause 6 might allow the domestic imposition of Convention liability on religious bodies which Strasbourg would not treat as bound by the Convention (or, more accurately, for whose actions the UK would not be liable at Strasbourg).[119] An additional government objection to the Lords' amendments was that in giving express protection to major religions[120] they might be found to

---

[116] HL Debs., 5 February 1998, cols. 805; amending cl. 6 (5).

[117] See also the decision of the Inner House of the Court of Session in *Ballantyre v Presbytery of Wigtown*, (1936), Session Cases (SC) 625, holding that the election of a minister by a congregation was an exclusively spiritual matter. See also *Logan v Presbytery of Dumbarton*, (1995), Scots Law Times (SLT) 1228, Ct. of Session – unsuccessful attempt at judicial review of disciplinary decisions of presbytery.

[118] Cl. 2(1) does not make the Strasbourg jurisprudence *binding* – UK courts are required to 'take into account' earlier decisions interpreting the Convention. Since many ECHR decisions on Arts. 8–11 turn upon the 'margin of appreciation' allowed to a member State in restricting Convention rights and this doctrine will not apply in the same way to domestic courts, it is to be expected that domestic judges will develop a distinct approach.

[119] An amendment designed to replicate the Convention jurisprudence under cl. 6 was unsuccessfully moved in the Committee stage: HC Debs., 17 June 1998, cols. 417–425.

[120] The reference to 'a Christian or other principal religious tradition represented in Great Britain' in cl. 7 (8) had been intended to overcome possible uncertainties over who might benefit from such a right. The sponsor (Baron-ness Young) made clear that she had in mind Christians, Jews, Muslims, Sikhs, Hindhus and Buddhists: HL Debs., 5 February 1998, col. 771. Similar wording appears in the Education Act 1996, s. 375 (n. 97, above).

discriminate contrary to Article 14 against other religions. This view was itself contentious: the Strasbourg organs have upheld preferential treatment for majority religions in earlier cases in certain circumstances. [121]

The government's response was to remove the Lords' amendments at the Committee Stage in the Commons and replace them with a new clause, reflecting in part the churches' concerns:

> If a court's determination of any question arising under this Act might affect the exercise by a religious organisation (itself or its members collectively) of the Convention right of freedom of thought, conscience and religion, it must have particular regard to the importance of that right. [122]

The clause was intended to meet concerns that Article 9 might be interpreted in an unduly individualistic way by the courts and so impede doctrinal decisions, hence the references to a 'religious organisation' (intended to embrace not just churches, but also religious charities and other religious non-charitable bodies) and to the collective exercise of rights. The Home Secretary conceded that the clause fell short of according automatic primacy to Article 9 over other rights, such as privacy or free speech, but argued that to do so would itself contravene the Convention. As it stands, the injunction to 'have particular regard to the importance of the right' points courts in that direction, without giving the absolute protection of an exemption or statutory defence.

The debate about religious liberty under the Human Rights Bill illustrates the difference between Liberal and Christian approaches discussed earlier. The campaign was met initially by the Lord Chancellor and human rights enthusiasts with disbelief that the churches should seek to exempt themselves from obligations to follow the Act. Critics argued that the incorporation of Article 9 was more than sufficient to protect freedom of religion and that specific exemptions were unnecessary. The failed attempt to obtain wholesale exemption for churches from the definition of a 'public authority' can be understood as an attempt to re-draw the proposed public/private divide so that all church activity was within the private sphere. This need not necessarily imply a rejection of the protection of religious liberty within the Liberal world-view: indeed, it draws its persuasive power from the Liberal approach discussed earlier that freedom of religion is a privatised matter. The argument was simply that the legislation had drawn the public/private boundary in the wrong place. Many non-conformists, who approach their churches as private voluntary associations, have an understandable difficulty in regarding them as 'public authorities' at all. The Home Secretary's later more mollient attempts to persuade the churches that few of their activities would fall within the public sphere

---

[121] see the *Otto-Preminger* and *Choudhury* cases at n. 74 and 77, above.
[122] New cl. 9. HC Debs., 20 May 1998, cols. 1013ff.

suggests that the campaign largely succeeded at the political level, although whether these reassurances are reflected in the decisions of the courts remains to be seen.

The amendments passed by the House of Lords were an attempt to preempt any future balancing exercise in which the courts might be called on to weigh freedom of religion against other clashing rights, by giving conclusiveness in the exempted situations to certain conscience argu - ments. From this viewpoint the amendments can be seen as highlighting the paradox of clashing rights within the Liberal perspective. They represented a refusal to be subject to a future balancing of rights by the judiciary, with the attendant risk that freedom of religion might be found not to apply[123] or might be outweighed by freedom from discrimination, etc. The new government clause which replaces these amendments and instructs the judges to pay particular regard to the importance of freedom of religion raises the same issue albeit in more obscure language intended to be Strasbourg-proof. Judicial balancing is, it seems, unavoidable within a Liberal framework, but the amendment means that the scales will be weighted in favour of freedom of religion.

IV. Conclusion

In this chapter I have argued that there are clear differences between Liberal and Christian approaches to religious liberty. Although initially derived from Christian writers, Liberal approaches now manifest a different emphasis characterised by a purported neutrality between relig - ions, the treatment of religion as a privatised and subjective matter, and intolerance towards intolerance. I have argued that from an external viewpoint this position fails to understand the nature of religious belief, except on its own terms, and lacks the neutrality which it claims to possess, and that from an internal perspective it embodies contradictory ap - proaches both to freedom of religion and to rights in general. A Christian approach to religious liberty, on the other hand, can be based on a specific understanding of the character of God and of human dignity and responsibility, involving *toleration* of those one believes to be wrong. Although it accords respect to freedom of conscience, for Christians religious liberty is not primarily a defensive posture within a hostile and secular environment: it is a positive freedom to work and witness freely.

On some issues (for example, the abolition of blasphemy) there may be convergence of outcomes between at least some of those advocating each approach, if for differing reasons. In other areas Christians will wish to assert an absolute right to manifest their religion where Liberals would argue it should be 'balanced' against or limited by some other right. In

---

[123] See pp. 44–45 above.

these areas Christians will be especially sceptical of Liberal claims to 'neutrality' in their approach and wary of the danger in enjoying religious freedom on the subordinating terms that it is private and not offensive to Liberals or to members of other religions or groups.

The Human Rights Act is the terrain on which these issues will be fought out in the future. It represents an opportunity for religious groups to carve out a positive right to manifest their religion for the first time in UK law as a valuable defence in an increasingly pluralistic and uncom - prehending society. However, it will also mean in effect that Christians who argue for legal recognition of religious freedom do so within what is an inherently Liberal mould of thought. The challenge will be to avoid compromise on the contradictions between it and the characteristics of Christian approaches. In a post-incorporation climate Christians will have to become adept at phrasing their political and moral arguments in the all-pervasive rights language of Liberals. Failure to do so will mean that the arguments are appropriated by other groups, with the danger that they are used to diminish religious freedom. The debates over the exemptions to the Human Rights Bill are the opening shots in what will probably prove to be a long campaign, and inevitably there will be legal reverses as well as successes. Absolute claims to religious liberty can be expected to expose some of the contradictions within the Liberal position. Like Paul in 'appealing to Rome'[124] Christians will be operating in a sphere which does not command their ultimate allegiance.

[124] See p. 48 above.

3

Why a Christian Philosophy of Law?

John Warwick Montgomery★

I. Introduction

Cardozo's essay on 'Law and Literature'[1] and Harvard jurisprudent Lon Fuller's imaginary cases in the mythical jurisdiction of Newgarth[2] offer adequate precedent for beginning with a fable.

Once upon a time a hare of philosophical temperament invited a politically orientated fox to dinner. During the entrée the hare presented an interesting argument on the relativity of all law and morals, stressing that each beast, in the final analysis, has a right to its own legal system. The fox did not find this argument entirely convincing on the intellectual level, but was much impressed with it practically. For dessert he ate the hare: *lapin à la crème*.

Moral: One's philosophical viewpoint can be of immense practical consequence, especially when the stakes (steaks?) are high.

II. The Need

First contact with the *Code of Professional Responsibility* of the American Bar Association[3] is a moving experience; here is a document reflecting

---

★ An earlier version of this essay appeared in Professor Montgomery's book, *The Law Above the Law*, (1975).

[1] B. Cardozo, 'Law and Literature', in *Essays on Jurisprudence from the Columbia Law Review*, (1963), 313.

[2] L. Fuller, 'The Problems of Jurisprudence', *passim* (1949). See also Fuller, 'The Case of the Speluncean Explorers', 62 *Harvard Law Review*, (1949), 616.

[3] The *Code* was adopted by the House of Delegates of the ABA on 12 August 12, 1969, to become effective on 1 January 1970; it has been amended on several occasions in subsequent years. The *Code* enlarges upon and officially replaces the ABA's *Canons of Professional Ethics*, adopted in 1908 and subsequently amended.

genuine concern to hold high the ethical standards of a great profession. Closer perusal of the *Code*, however, elicits a sense of growing disquiet. Not that the standards are wrong; but what precisely do they *mean* at the points of fundamental ethical commitment? 'A lawyer . . . should be temperate and dignified, and he should refrain from all illegal and morally reprehensible conduct.'[4] To question such affirmations would seem, on one level, as sacrilegious as doubting motherhood or the flag; but is this not precisely their danger? They use the right words, but they do not define them; they continually beg the question of who, specifi - cally, is to set the standards of 'temperance' and 'dignity' and who is to say when conduct is indeed 'morally reprehensible'. The practical consequences of such vagueness are most serious. A penetrating analysis of 'Law Schools and Ethics' points out that the profession's standards do not, for example, make plain whether a lawyer *need not* or *must not* 'do for his client that which the lawyer thinks is unfair, unconscionable, or overreaching, even if lawful'.[5]

Throughout the *Code* emphasis is placed upon conduct which shall deserve the approval of peers. '[I]n the last analysis it is the desire for the respect and confidence of the members of his profession and of the society which he serves that should provide to a lawyer the incentive for the highest possible degree of ethical conduct. The possible loss of that respect and confidence is the ultimate sanction'.[6] Here the dubious assumption is made that society will somehow maintain that undefined high standard of which the Code speaks. The realistic possibility is never faced that standards – even the standards of an entire society – can decline or disappear.

Interestingly enough, the American *Uniform Commercial Code* (hardly a document replete with philosophical insights) displays uncomfortable awareness of this grim possibility. In the official comment relating to course of dealing and usage of trade we read: '[T]he anciently established policing of usage by the courts is continued to the extent necessary to cope with the situation arising if an unconscionable or dishonest practice should become standard'.[7] The Watergate tragedy is an appalling example

---

[4]   ABA *Code of Professional Responsibility*, EC 1–5.

[5]   M.L. Schwartz, 'Law Schools and Ethics', *Chronicle of Higher Education*, 9 December 1974, at 20; cf. ABA *Canons of Professional Ethics* No. 15: The attorney 'must obey his own conscience and not that of his client' (see also No. 18). But what value system is to inform the attorney's conscience? '[N]o client has a right to demand that his counsel shall be illiberal, or that he do anything therein repugnant to his own sense of honor and propriety' (No. 24; cf. No. 44). 'Illiberal' by what criterion? 'Honour' and 'propriety' by whose definition?

[6]   ABA *Code of Professional Responsibility*, Preamble. See also ABA *Canons*, No. 32.

[7]   *Uniform Commercial Code*, s. 1–205, Comment 6.

of the ease with which societal standards can in fact deteriorate – and it is noteworthy that this occurred in an administration relying more than any previous one on the services of lawyers and the legally trained.

How precisely correct was the judgement of the US Supreme Court in a case of personal influence upon public officials exactly one hundred years before Watergate:

> The foundation of a republic is the virtue of its citizens. They are at once sovereigns and subjects. As the foundation is undermined, the structure is weakened. When it is destroyed, the fabric must fall. Such is the voice of universal history. Montesquieu *Spirit of Laws*, 17.

> If the instances [of selling influence to procure privately advantageous legislation] were numerous, open and tolerated, they would be regarded as measuring the decay of the public morals and the degeneracy of the times. No prophetic spirit would be needed to foretell the consequences near at hand.[8]

When public morals decay and the times degenerate, of what consequence is society's approval or reputation for ethical action? If all Cretans are liars, is it a compliment to be praised by a Cretan? And in such a situation, what is the individual or collective conscience necessarily worth? Conscience is environmentally conditioned, and the morals of the time will influence what is regarded as conscionable or unconscionable. Among cannibals, one feels guilty for not cleaning one's plate.

The problem of establishing sound ethical standards in the legal profession and the wider problem of which this is but one aspect – that of finding ethical norms for the evaluation of positive law in general – becomes immensely more acute when we see total societies operating with legal and ethical values directly opposed to our own. Solzhenitsyn, in *The Gulag Archipelago*, eloquently and passionately condemns the dehumanisation of the individual in the juridical 'sewage disposal system' of Marxist Russia,[9] and his argument has been documented *ad nauseam* by others;[10] yet none of this impresses the Marxist-Leninist jurisprudent, who simply quotes Lenin's fundamental rule of socialist legal philosophy: 'We have no more private law, for with us all has become public law.'[11] In the temporary 'dictatorship of the proletariat' prior to the onset of the

---

8 *Trist* v *Child*, 88 US (21 Wall.), 441 (1874), (J. Swayne).

9 A. Solzhenitsyn, *The Gulag Archipelago 1918–1956*, pt. 1 (1974); cf. J.B. Dunlop, R. Haugh and A. Klimoff (eds.), *A. Solzhenitsyn: Critical Essays and Documentary Materials*, (1973).

10 E.g. International Commission of Jurists, *Justice Enslaved: A Collection of Documents on the Abuse of Justice for Political Ends*, (1955).

11 See V.I. Lenin, *et al.*, *Soviet Legal Philosophy, passim* (20th Century Legal Philosophy Ser. Vol. 5, 1951); cf. R. David and J. Brierley, *Major Legal Systems in the World Today*, (1968), 157–58.

idyllic classless (communist) society, the law exists pragmatically as an instrument of socialist policy;[12] and following Lenin's ethic that the end justifies the means,[13] the disregard of due process and the consequent miseries of political defendants and prisoners under the Soviet legal system were straightforwardly justified as furthering State interests.

Or consider National Socialist legal operations in the Germany of the 1930s and 1940s. After observing the situation in Nazi Germany at firsthand, Dr William Burdick of the University of Kansas Law Faculty wrote in 1939:

> It is a necessary part of the machinery of dictatorships that the law and the courts shall be subservient to the ruler. In 1933, it was officially declared in Germany that the final authority as to the principles of the State and the law is the National Socialist German Workers' Party; that no other political party could be formed; and that the Fuehrer should make its laws. Does this declaration differ in principle from the decree of Soviet Russia stating that the 'Socialist Conscience' shall be the final arbiter? Today, in Germany all judges are not only appointed by the present government but they are also subject to dismissal by arbitrary power. As a result, all Hebrew judges, of which there were a considerable number, many of them being Germany's ablest jurists, have been dismissed from all the courts. Moreover, this 'purge' has not been limited to the judicial profession, it has been extended to the lawyers also. In 1933, the former German Bar Association was dissolved, and a National Socialist Lawyers Society was established in its place. All its members must be of German blood, and by official decree a person is not considered to be of German blood if his parents or grand-parents have Jewish blood in their veins. It was further decreed that all public officials of non-Aryan descent should be retired. This included judges, lawyers, counsellors in administrative law, consultants on cases in the labor courts, court officials, and candidates in training for the judicial or legal professions. In 1933, twenty-seven percent of all the lawyers in Berlin were of Jewish blood. Their citizenship has been taken away and with it their right to vote. No additional Jewish lawyers can be trained, because all Jews are now excluded from the German universities.[14]

As we are well aware, the sufferings of the legal profession in Germany were paralleled at every level of the society, and in the apocalyptic holocaust of the Third Reich six million Jews perished.

After the Nazi defeat the blood of these victims cried out for justice; war crimes trials were an inevitability. But what standard was to be used at Nuremberg to judge the accused leaders of the Nazi regime? When the Charter of the Tribunal, which had been drawn up by the victors, was used by the prosecution, the defendants very logically complained

---

[12]   See J.W. Montgomery, *The Shape of the Past*, (1963), 74, 80, 217.

[13]   Cf. J. Fletcher and J.W. Montgomery, *Situation Ethics: True or False*, (1972), 79, 82, 83.

[14]   W.L. Burdick, *The Bench and Bar of Other Lands*, (1939), 422.

that they were being tried under *ex post facto* laws; and some authorities in the field of international law have severely criticised the allied judges on the same ground.[15] The most telling defence offered by the accused was that they had simply followed orders or made decisions within the framework of their own legal system, in complete consistency with it, and that they therefore could not rightly be condemned because they deviated from the alien value system of their conquerors. Faced with this argument, Robert H. Jackson, Chief Counsel for the United States at the trials, was compelled to appeal to permanent values, to moral standards transcending the life-styles of particular societies – in a word, to a 'law beyond the law' of individual nations, whether victor or vanquished:

> It is common to think of our own time as standing at the apex of civilization, from which the deficiencies of preceding ages may patronizingly be viewed in the light of what is assumed to be 'progress.' The reality is that in the long perspective of history the present century will not hold an admirable position, unless its second half is to redeem its first. These two-score years in this twentieth century will be recorded in the book of years as one of the most bloody in all annals. Two World Wars have left a legacy of dead which number more than all the armies engaged in any war that made ancient or medieval history. No half-century ever witnessed slaughter on such a scale, such cruelties and inhumanities, such wholesale deportations of peoples into slavery, such annihilations of minorities. The terror of Torquemada pales before the Nazi inquisition. These deeds are the overshadowing historical facts by which generations to come will remember this decade. If we cannot eliminate the causes and prevent the repetition of these barbaric events, it is not an irresponsible prophecy to say that this twentieth century may yet succeed in bringing the doom of civilization.
>
> Goaded by these facts, we have moved to redress the blight on the record of our era . . .
>
> . . . At this stage of the proceedings, I shall rest upon the law of these crimes as laid down in the Charter . . .
>
> In interpreting the Charter, however, we should not overlook the unique and emergent character of this body as an International Military Tribunal. It is no part of the constitutional mechanism of internal justice of any of the Signatory nations . . . As an International Military Tribunal, it rises above the provincial and transient and seeks guidance not only from International Law but also from the basic principles of jurisprudence which are assumptions of civilization . . .[16]

[15] E.g. George A. Finch and Professor Edwin Borchard, 41 *American Journal of International Law*, (1947), 20, 107, 334; cf. R. Wormser, *The Story of the Law*, (rev. ed., 1962), 557.

[16] R. Jackson, 'Closing Address in the Nuremberg Trial', in 19 *Proceedings in the Trial of the Major War Criminals Before the International Military Tribunal* , (1948), 397. For valuable bibliographical references on the Nuremberg trial, see W. Bishop, *International Law*, (3rd ed., 1971), 996, 1016–18.

Thus have the horrors of our recent history forced us to recognise the puerile inadequacy of tying ultimate legal standards to the mores of a particular society, even if that society is our own. To 'redress the blight on the record of our era' demands nothing less than a recovery of those 'basic principles of jurisprudence which are assumptions of civilization'.

III. The Dilemma

But where are the basic principles of 'higher law' to be found, and how are they to be identified and justified? *Voilà* the great dilemma: for however much our world cries out for absolute values of rightness, they seem forever beyond our grasp. Like Ponce de León's *ciudad de oro*, the permanent legal norms for which we search appear always to lie on the other side of the next mountain.

And yet every day, in every court of the land, decisions are handed down in reliance on 'higher' principles which do not themselves derive from precedent. H.L.A. Hart correctly observes that 'because precedents can logically be assumed under an indefinite number of general rules, the identification of *the* rule for which a precedent is an authority cannot be settled by an appeal to logic'.[17] The same point is made in detail by A.W.B. Simpson, through analysis of the leading English tort liability case of *Rylands* v *Fletcher*[18] (*held*: one is liable at his peril for the natural and probable consequences of the escape of any potentially dangerous thing which he has brought upon his land) and its qualification in *Nichols* v *Marsland*[19] (*held*: defendant not liable, since an extraordinary rain caused his reservoir to overflow and flood plaintiff's land).

> [W]hen, for example, the case of *Nichols* v *Marsland* was distinguished from *Rylands* v *Fletcher* upon the ground that the escape was caused by an act of God, the court's acceptance of this distinction did involve some recognition of some justificatory principle of morality, justice, social policy or common-sense which was external to the law, and this will generally be found to be the case when law is made. For though the making of law may be justified by legal rules which permit the making of laws by this or that person upon this or that occasion, the content of the law which is so made requires a different type of justification.[20]

---

[17] H.L.A. Hart, 'Philosophy of Law, Problems of', in 6 *Encyclopedia of Philosophy*, (P. Edwards, ed., 1967), 264, 270.

[18] L.R. 3 H.L. 330, (1868).

[19] 2 Ex. D. 1, (1876).

[20] A.W.B. Simpson, 'The "Ratio Decidendi" of a Case and the Doctrine of Binding Precedent, in A.G. Guest (ed.), *Oxford Essays in Jurisprudence* (First Ser.), (2nd ed., 1968), 148, 175.

But what is this 'different type of justification'? We have seen that the precedents of the case law do not necessarily yield it. As C.J. Bartley, argued in reversing a *nisi prius* decision based on a well-established rule of accord and satisfaction in the law of contracts: 'When we consider the thousands of cases to be pointed out in the English and American books of reports, which have been overruled, doubted, or limited in their application, we can appreciate the remark of Chancellor Kent in his *Commentaries*, Vol. 1, page 477, that "Even a series of decisions are not always evidence of what the law is".'[21] Professor Corbin of Yale, who includes this case in his standard text, *Cases on the Law of Contracts*, appends to Bartley's opinion this question for the student: 'A precedent seems not to be conclusive. What is?'[22] What, indeed?

Equity lawyers have tended to locate the 'higher law' within the sphere of Chancery; yet legal history plainly shows that courts of equity, though they have often corrected the rigidities and injustices of the law courts, are subject to parallel arteriosclerosis.[23] The legislatively minded and the devotees of the continental Civil Law tradition see statute as the modern way to introduce justice into the fusty tradition created by anachronistic case law; but statutory injustice and stupidity are at least as manifest as the evils of bad precedent (one thinks of a Kansas statute that changed the meaning of π from 3.1416 to an even 3, and another that declared: 'When two trains approach each other at a crossing, they shall both come to a full stop, and neither shall start up until the other has gone').[24]

Other jurisprudents have attempted to penetrate behind case law, equity, and statute to some fundamental notion capable of supplying the needed permanent criterion of legal worth: Volansky, operating in the French tradition, suggests the jural concept of 'good faith',[25] much in the spirit of the *Uniform Commercial Code*, which places central emphasis on this same concept.[26] Lord Radcliffe, in his 1960 Rosenthal Lectures, after admitting that 'you cannot hope to get Natural Law in at the front door', tries to get it in at the back by way of the principle of 'public interest' or

---

[21] *Leavitt* v *Morrow*, 6 Ohio St. 71, 67 Am. Dec. 334, (1856).

[22] A. Corbin, *Cases on the Law of Contracts*, (3rd ed., 1947), 916.

[23] Cf. A.V. Dicey, *Law & Public Opinion in England During the 19th Century*, (2nd ed., 1914, reissued 1962), 375–82, and Lord Justice James' remarks on the oppressive character of older Chancery pleadings: *Davy* v *Garrett*, 38 L.T.R. (m.s.) 81, (1878).

[24] J.A. Duncan, *The Strangest Cases on Record*, (1940), 183–84; cf. B. Warée, *Curiosités judiciaires*, (1859), 385–98.

[25] A. Volansky, *Essai d'une définition expressive du Droit basée sur l'idée de bonne foi*, (1930).

[26] See *Uniform Commercial Code* ss. 1–203; 2–209, Comment 2; 2–305, Comment 6; 2–306, Comment 1; 2–309, Comment 5; etc.

'public policy'.[27] Yet like the ABA *Code's* notions of 'temperance', 'dignity', and 'the respect of society', these concepts remain vague and undefined – open to all possibilities of definition and redefinition by the society of the moment. What standard of justice would the concept of 'good faith' offer in a Marxist-Leninist culture, where the end is held to justify the means? Would we be satisfied with the justice of 'public policy' under National Socialism? In point of fact, such maximally generalised legal notions are like the chameleon: they take their colour from the societal pattern and are incapable of arresting degeneracy in the society at large or in the legal sphere in particular.

To compound the difficulty in the search for 'higher law', some of the most influential jurisprudents and philosophers of our time have con-cluded that a solution to this problem is impossible in principle. H.L.A. Hart, after perceptively distinguishing between the 'primary rules' of social obligation and the 'secondary rules' by which a structure of positive law is created, identifies the ultimate secondary rule as the 'rule of recognition' – the criterion by which law is recognised to be such in a society. When the question is raised as to the validity of a given society's rule of recognition (e.g. we might think of Nazi Germany's refusal to recognise Jews as persons deserving of legal rights), Hart answers:

> We only need the word 'validity', and commonly only use it, to answer questions which arise within a system of rules where the status of a rule as a member of the system depends on its satisfying certain criteria provided by the rule of recognition. No such question can arise as to the validity of the very rule of recognition which provides the criteria; it can neither be valid nor invalid but is simply accepted as appropriate for use in this way.[28]

Thus each society's ultimate legal foundations are uncriticisable, since any criticism could only come from another society whose rules of recognition have no more absolute validity than those of the society being criticised.

Hans Kelsen argues in a similar vein that each legal system is a hierarchical structure (*Stufenbau*), grounded in a basic norm (*Grundnorm*). This basic norm gives coherence to the plurality of legal principles in the system and keeps it from disintegration. But the question as to the ultimate validity of the *Grundnorm* is unanswerable.

> It is of the greatest importance to be aware of the fact that there is not only one moral or political system, but at different times and within different

---

27 Lord Radcliffe, *The Law and Its Compass: 1960 Rosenthal Lectures, Northwestern University School of Law* (1961), 33, 57.

28 H.L.A. Hart, *The Concept of Law*, (Oxford 1965), 105–106; cf. 'Symposium: The Philosophy of H.L.A. Hart', in 35 *University of Chicago Law Review*, (1967), 1; 'Philosophies du droit anglaises et américaines', in 15 *Archives de la Philosophie du Droit*, (1970), 113, 179; and R. Sartorius, 'Hart's Concept of Law', in R. Summers (ed.), *More Essays in Legal Philosophy*, (1971), 131.

societies several very different moral and political systems are considered to be valid by the men living under these normative systems. These systems actually came into existence by custom, or by commands of outstanding personalities like Moses, Jesus or Mohammed. If men believe that these personalities are inspired by a transcendental, supernatural – that is a divine authority – the moral or political system has a religious character. It is especially in this case when the moral or political system is supposed to be of divine origin that the values constituted by it are considered to be absolute. If, however, the fact is taken into consideration that there are, there were and probably always will be several different moral and political systems actually presupposed to be valid within different societies, the values constituted by these systems can be considered to be only of a relative character; then the judgment that a definitive government or a definite legal order is just can be pronounced only with reference to one of the several different political and moral systems, and then the same behaviour or the same governmental activity or the same legal order may with reference to another moral or political system be considered as morally bad or as politically unjust.[29]

The implications of such a viewpoint are patently horrifying (Nuremberg trials are ruled out in principle and the foxes of this world can eat the hares as a regular diet), but the logical problems in establishing absolute legal norms are equally formidable. How exactly can a given society or a given individual transcend the values of the culture so as to arrive at standards of absolute worth? In the nineteenth century Søren Kierkegaard, the father of modern existentialism, rightly castigated and ridiculed the pretentious philosophical idealism of Hegel. Was it con - ceivable, he asked, that one man should be able to disengage himself from the human predicament – shed his own skin – to the point of seeing the World Spirit of Reason carry the human race dialectically to perfect freedom? Hegel had asserted that history would pass through four 'world-historical' epochs, concluding with the 'Germanic'; his perspec - tive here turned out to be the product of the rising German nationalism of his time, not a judgement of universal validity.[30] But who – whether idealistic Hegelian, materialistic Marxist, or Western liberal jurisprudent – could see all of history so as to establish its total meaning, or survey and sift the universe of values so as to declare absolute legal and moral principle? As humorist and lay 'philosopher' Woody Allen succinctly put

---

29   Lecture delivered by Hans Kelsen at the University of California, 20 November 1962 (tape at Boalt Hall Library); cf. R.G. Decker, 'The Secularization of Anglo-American Law: 1800–1970', in 49 *Thought*, (1974), 280, 292–93, 297; A.S. de Bustamante y Montoro, 'Kelsenism', in P. Sayre (ed.), *Interpretations of Modern Legal Philosophies: Essays in Honor of Roscoe Pound*, (1947), 43; and M.P. Golding, 'Kelsen and the Concept of "Legal System" ', in R. Summers (ed.), *More Essays in Legal Philosophy*, (1971), 69.

30   See J.W. Montgomery, *Where is History Going?*, (1969), 15–36.

it: 'Can we actually "know" the universe? My God, it's hard enough finding your way around in Chinatown.'[31]

Contemporary analytical philosophers, though lacking in Woody Allen's pungency of expression, have made the same point with logical rigor. Wittgenstein, in his famed *Tractatus*, argued that our societal and personal limits as human beings forever keep us from producing absolute philosophies that are indeed absolute: 'The sense of the world must lie outside the world . . . And so it is impossible for there to be propositions of ethics . . . Ethics is transcendental'.[32] Metaphorically expanding on this theme in his posthumously published 'Lecture on Ethics', Wittgenstein says:

> [W]e cannot write a scientific book, the subject matter of which could be intrinsically sublime and above all other subject matters. I can only describe my feeling by the metaphor, that, if a man could write a book on Ethics which really was a book on Ethics, this book would, with an explosion, destroy all the other books in the world.[33]

To arrive at absolute legal standards, one would have to disengage oneself from the world and its limited standards and go 'outside the world' to a 'transcendental' realm of values. Only there could the 'intrinsically sublime' hornbook be found. To be sure, this is entirely in accord with common sense. Water does not rise above its own level; why should we think that absolute legal norms will arise from relativistic human situations? Archimedes said that if he were given a lever long enough and a fulcrum outside the world he could move it. Quite right; but all depends on a fulcrum *outside* the world. The very expressions '*higher* law' and 'law *beyond* the law' are suggestive of this, for they employ transcendental qualifiers.[34] The essential first step in the quest for absolute legal norms is the recognition that – however much we need them and want them – we will never find them by building jurisprudential towers of Babel.

Rousseau, who did not generally display such philosophical perception, formulated the dilemma with stark accuracy in his description of the work of the legislator:

> In order to discover the rules of society best suited to nations, a superior intelligence beholding all the passions of men without experiencing any of them would be needed. This intelligence would have to be wholly unrelated to our nature, while knowing it through and through; its happiness would have to be independent of us, and yet ready to occupy itself with ours; and lastly, it would have, in the march of time, to look forward to a distant glory,

31   W. Allen, 'My Philosophy', in *The New Yorker*, 27 December 1969, at 25.
32   L. Wittgenstein, *Tractatus Logico-Philosophicus*, ss. 6.41–6.421.
33   Wittgenstein, 'Lecture on Ethics', 74 *Philosophy Review*, (1965), 3, 7.
34   Cf. I.T. Ramsey, *Religious Language*, (1957), *passim*.

and, working in one century, to be able to enjoy in the next. It would take gods to give men laws. . .[35]

IV. The Solution

The traditional answer to the cruel dilemma of desperately needing 'higher law' yet not being humanly capable of creating it, is Natural Law theory. The essence of this theory, which held sway from classical Greek times to the French Revolution and which is experiencing a significant revival today,[36] is that absolute ethical standards and fundamental legal rightness are implanted in the human situation and can be discovered as the common elements in the moral codes and positive legislation of all men and cultures. Such Natural Law was formerly regarded as a product and evidence of God's hand in the world. In the words of Cicero:

> I find that it has been the opinion of the wisest men that Law is not a product of human thought, nor is it any enactment of peoples, but something eternal which rules the whole universe by its wisdom in command and prohibition. Thus they have been accustomed to say that Law is the primal and ultimate mind of God . . .[37]

But what precisely is the 'something eternal' in the laws of mankind, and how is it to be distinguished from the merely human, temporal and ephemeral? This is a question of cardinal importance, for unless a clear distinction can be made it will obviously be impossible to criticise any given positive law on the basis of something more fundamental: what is considered 'eternal' may turn out to be no more than 'temporal' and thus subject to the same difficulties as what is being criticised.

Here is the crux of the problem in all Natural Law thinking. If the Natural Law is stated in typically classic terms – for example, in the

---

[35] J.-J. Rousseau, *Contrat social*, bk. 2, ch. 7.

[36] 'The revival of natural-law doctrines is one of the most interesting features of current legal thought' – M.P. Golding, 'Philosophy of Law, History of', in 6 *Encyclopedia of Philosophy* 254, 263, (P. Edwards, ed., 1967). Cf. J. Charmont, *La Renaissance du Droit naturel*, (2nd ed., 1927); C.G. Haines, *The Revival of Natural Law Concepts*, (Harv. Studies in Juris, Vol. 4, reprint ed., 1965); J. Cogley, R.M. Hutchins, *et al.*, *Natural Law and Modern Society*, (1966); F. Castberg, *La Philosophie du Droit*, (1970); J. Finnis, *Natural Law and Natural Rights*, (Oxford, 1980); and Gianformaggio's article 'Droit naturel', with bibliography, in the *Dictionnaire encyclopédique de théorie et de sociologie du droit*, 198 (2nd ed., A.-J. Arnaud, 1993). For a detailed expression of traditional Natural Law theory, see Th. Jouffroy, *Cours du droit naturel*, (5th ed., 1876).

[37] M.T. Cicero, *De Legibus*, bk. 2, ch. 4.

formula of the Justinian Code, 'Honeste vivere, neminem laedere, suum cuique tribuere' (live honestly, harm no one, give to each his own) [38] – it is, as Harvard's C.J. Friedrich observes, so 'imprecise' that it does little more than to underscore the need for 'some kind of equity'. [39] When attempts have been made to specify the Natural Law in more concrete terms, the results have been either a listing of ethical and legal principles common to diverse cultures [40] (entailing the fallacious assumption, known as the 'naturalistic fallacy', that what is universal is necessarily right) or an attribution of eternal value to positions, such as the Roman Catholic condemnation of 'unnatural' methods of birth control, that are highly disputable. [41]

The most sophisticated of current Natural Law thinkers – those influenced by the analytical movement in philosophy – have been able to identify certain fundamental, trans-cultural ethical and legal demands imposed upon us by our humanity. L.H. Perkins argues, for example:

> The use of language implies a commitment as much as life in society does – a commitment to communicate, i.e. to use that language in a way that others may understand if they too are users of that language; i.e. to use that language properly. Thus, Jones has an obligation to follow through on that promise he made to Smith, and so does an anarchist who opposes the whole institution of promising – the obligation is built into the language, which is built into the institution, and the institution is built into nature by the fact that man is a political, i.e. an institutional, animal . . . [42]

The reasoning here is impeccable, but it does not go beyond the most general obligations (truth-telling, keeping promises) – obligations of a heuristic or necessitarian character that are incapable of fleshing out the skeleton of Natural Law. [43] Specifically, what *kind* of contractual obligations should be enforced at law? Promises by cannibals, based on adequate consideration, to clean their plates? It should give pause that the vague expression of the *Digest*, 'Give to each his own', was inscribed in German translation ('Jedem das seine') on the metal doors leading into Buchenwald. [44]

---

[38]   Cf. A. d'Entrèves, *Natural Law*, (2nd ed., 1970), 22.

[39]   C.J. Friedrich, *The Philosophy of Law in Historical Perspective*, (2nd ed., 1963), 22.

[40]   A useful list is provided in C.S. Lewis, *The Abolition of Man*, (1947), 51.

[41]   Cf. J.W. Montgomery, 'How to Decide the Birth Control Question', in W. Spitzer and C. Saylor (eds.), *Birth Control and the Christian*, (1969), 575.

[42]   L.H. Perkins, 'Natural Law in Contemporary Analytic Philosophy', 17 *American Journal of Jurisprudence*, (1972), 111, 118.

[43]   Cf. G. Del Vecchio's argument that veracity constitutes a juridical obligation: *La Justice – La Vérité: Essais de philosophie juridique et morale*, (1955), 173, 195, 231.

[44]   Personal observation of the author.

In the Preface to his classic *The Revival of Natural Law Concepts*, Haines singles out this vagueness as the prime characteristic of Natural Law theories: 'Carlyle, in speaking of the views of the Roman jurists on natural law, doubted whether any of the lawyers had very clear conceptions upon the matter. As a matter of fact all theories of natural law have a singular vagueness . . .'[45] Is there any way of overcoming this fatal flaw?

Considerable aid in solving the problem comes from the approach taken by a certain law-trained first-century theologian in his confronta-tion with Stoic philosophers. The Stoics had provided the basic formu-lation of Roman Natural Law theory and it was from them that the great classical thinkers (Cicero, Seneca *et al.*) derived their views on the subject.[46] Thus it is most instructive to observe an early corrective to the vagueness of these views.

[C]ertain Epicurean and Stoic philosophers encountered [Paul at Athens]. And some said, What will this babbler say? Others said, He seems to be setting forth strange gods – for he had been preaching Jesus and the resurrection to them. And they took him to the Areopagus, saying, May we know what this new doctrine is of which you are speaking? . . .

Then Paul stood at the center of the Areopagus and said, You men of Athens, I note that in all things you are too superstitious. For as I passed by and beheld your devotions, I found an altar with this inscription: TO THE UNKNOWN GOD. Whom therefore you ignorantly worship I declare to you . . . [T]he times of this ignorance God winked at, but now commands all men everywhere to repent, for he has appointed a day when he will judge the world in righteousness by the Man whom he has ordained, and he has given assurance of it to all in that he has raised him from the dead.[47]

It is the conviction of the apostle Paul that natural religion – man's search for ultimate values – is correct as far as it goes, but it does not go far enough. This search arrives at some notion of ultimacy, but its content is 'unknown' – and would always have remained unknown if God in his mercy had not specifically revealed himself in the biblical history of salvation which culminates in the death and resurrection of Jesus Christ. 'Whom therefore you ignorantly worship I declare to you.'

As applied to the issue of legal values, the vague generalities of Natural Law are made concrete and visible through a specific scriptural revelation of the divine will for man. (The law was given through Moses; grace and

---

[45] C.G. Haines, *supra*, n. 36, at vii.

[46] See T.E Holland, *The Elements of Jurisprudence*, (13th ed., 1924), 33; and cf. E. Zeller, *Outlines of the History of Greek Philosophy*, (13th ed., W. Nestle, 1931), 209, 266, and his *Stoics, Epicureans, and Sceptics*, (1870).

[47] Acts 17:18–19, 22–23, 30–31. It is noteworthy that in v. 28 Paul quotes Stoic philosophical poetry; the reference is almost certainly to Cleanthes' 'Hymn to Zeus' – text in *Essential Works of Stoicism*, (M. Hadas, ed., 1965), 51.

truth came through Jesus Christ.) [48] Wittgenstein's 'intrinsically sublime' book of ethics actually exists; Archimedes' fulcrum outside the world is a reality, so the world of human values can in fact be moved; [49] Rousseau's 'superior intelligence' as legislator is not a mere ideal – and instead of being coldly 'unrelated to our nature' and without 'experience of the passions of men', God himself entered our midst, was 'like us yet without sin', [50] and imparted to us the true nature and fulfilment of eternal law.

But why should such a stupendous claim be accepted? And what about competing claims to divinely revealed law, such as that of the Muslims? [51] Admittedly (and students of the law ought to be the first to recognise it) to make a claim is hardly to prove a case; in the realm of ultimate values no less than in the sphere of legal issues, competing claims must be arbitrated by factual evidence. It is precisely at this evidential point that the biblical revelation stands vindicated in com - parison with all other such claims. [52] Doubtless this is why so many great legal scholars have been prominent apologists – defenders – of the biblical 'higher law'. Space forbids an analysis of their arguments here except for a brief mention of especially noteworthy examples: [53] Hugo Grotius, the 'father of international law', whose *De veritate religionis Christianae* (On the Truth of the Christian Religion, 1627) stressed the reliability of the gospel accounts of Jesus' life; Simon Greenleaf, Royall Professor of Law at Harvard and the greatest American authority on Common Law evidence in the nineteenth century, whose *Testimony of the Evangelists*[54] establishes the New Testament as documentary evidence acceptable to the courts – admissible and competent relative to its substantive claims concerning Jesus' person and work; J.N.D. Anderson, late Professor of Oriental Laws and Director of the Institute of Advanced Legal Studies in the University of London, whose *Christianity: The*

---

[48] Jn. 1:17.

[49] Cf. Acts 17:6, where the early preachers of the gospel are referred to by their opponents as 'those who have turned the world upside down'.

[50] Heb. 4:15.

[51] R. David and J. Brierley, *supra* note 11, at 386: '. . . Muslim jurists and theologians have built up a complete and detailed law on the basis of divine revelation [the Koran] – the law of an ideal society which one day will be established in a world entirely subject to Islamic religion'.

[52] See J.W. Montgomery, 'The Apologetic Approach of Muhammad Ali and Its Implications for Christian Apologetics', 51 *Muslim World*, (1961), 111; cf. Corrigendum in July 1961 *Muslim World*.

[53] For other important examples, together with detailed discussion of the arguments briefly mentioned here, see J.W. Montgomery, *Jurisprudence: A Book of Readings*, (1974), *passim*.

[54] Greenleaf's seminal essay is included as an Appendix in J.W. Montgomery, *The Law Above the Law*, (1975), with the typographical errors of earlier editions corrected.

Witness of History and *The Evidence for the Resurrection*[55] demonstrate the facticity of Jesus' resurrection from the dead, and with it the truth of his claim to be no less than God incarnate and the soundness of his declarations that the Old Testament law derives from God himself and faithfully reflects the divine will.

When analysed by the most rigorous standards of historical scholarship and by the most exacting canons of legal evidence, the accounts of Jesus in the New Testament are found to be the very opposite of hearsay; they are primary-source records produced by eyewitnesses.[56] 'We have not followed cunningly devised myths', the writers consistently maintain, 'when we made known to you the power and coming of our Lord Jesus Christ, but were eyewitnesses of his majesty.'[57] If testimony is worth anything – and our entire legal operation is nothing without it – then the case for biblically revealed 'higher law' is established not merely by the preponderance of evidence required in civil actions but to 'a moral certainty, to the exclusion of all reasonable doubt'.[58] The test was well stated by C.J. Shaw, in the classic case of *Commonwealth* v *Webster*: '[T]he circumstances taken as a whole, and giving them their reasonable and just weight, and no more, should to a moral certainty exclude every other hypothesis'.[59] How precise is the application of this test to the evidential case for 'higher law' offered by the apostolic company: Jesus 'through the Holy Spirit gave commandments to the apostles whom he had chosen – to whom also he showed himself alive after his passion by many infallible proofs . . .'[60]

V. Benefits to the Prodigal Lawyer

If revelational 'higher law' can indeed be established as a permanent arbiter of the positive law, two questions remain: first, what are its benefits? and, second, why has modern man – and the modern lawyer in particular – departed from it?

[55] These works can be obtained from, respectively, Tyndale Press, 39 Bedford Sq., London, and Inter-Varsity Press, Downers Grove, Ill., USA.

[56] J.W. Montgomery, *History and Christianity*, (1970); Montgomery, 'Legal Reasoning and Christian Apologetics', in *Christianity Today*, 14 February 1975.

[57] 2 Pet. 1:16.

[58] The classic formulation of T. Starkie: 1 *Law of Evidence*, (2nd ed., 1833), 478; cf. Wigmore, *Treatise on Evidence*, s. 2497. See also J. Gambier, *Moral Evidence* (3rd ed., 1824), and A. Bucknill, *The Nature of Evidence*, (1953).

[59] *Commonwealth* v *Webster*, 59 Mass. (5 Cush.) 295, 52 Am. Dec. 711, (1850). Cf. L.W. Levy, 'The Law of the Commonwealth and Chief Justice Shaw' (1957, reprinted 1967), 218–28.

[60] Acts 1:1–3.

The benefits of an explicit, divine standard of justice ramify through all areas of human life. We shall mention here four of the principal advantages of the biblical 'higher law'.

(1) *An explicit, non-question-begging standard of absolute justice is provided, by which the evil laws of sinful men and of sinful societies can be evaluated and corrected.* No longer is one at the mercy of the vague and undefined idealism of professional codes or Natural Law theories, whose terminol - ogy ('honesty', 'dignity', 'temperance') can be twisted in virtually any direction. No longer is one caught in the vice of societal standards – which can (and do) deteriorate under the pressures of modern life. Why should Jews and Blacks and members of other minority groups receive equal protection under the law? Why was Nazi racism juridically dam - nable? Not because of our current Western social values – since these have no more permanence or absolute validity than those of other peoples – but because God Almighty has declared once and for all that he has 'made of one blood all nations of men to dwell on all the face of the earth' and that 'there is neither Jew nor Greek, there is neither bond nor free'.[61] Thus is human equality and legal standing regardless of race or colour established on the rock of 'higher law', above the shifting sands of cultural change. Thomas Mann has magnificently captured the wonder and inestimable value of such revealed law:

> [A]ll the people came before Moses that he might give them what he had brought: the message of Jahwe from the mountain, the tables with the decalogue.
>
> 'Take them, O blood of my father', he said, 'and keep them holy in God's tent. But that which they say, that keep holy yourselves in doing and in leaving undone. For it is the brief and binding, the condensed will of God, the bed-rock of all good behaviour and breeding, and God wrote it in the stone with my little graving tool – the Alpha and Omega of human decency . . .'[62]

(2) *Biblically revealed 'higher law' offers the only reliable guide to personal and national health, and thus to the preservation of individual and corporate life* . The 'thousand-year Reich' that idolatrously arrogated divine functions to itself and ignored God's revealed law perished in a generation, 'and great was

---

[61]   Acts 17:26; Gal. 3:28. Space limitations preclude our dealing here with the hermeneutical question of which Old Testament commands are applicable to all human societies and not just to ancient Israel as a special vehicle of God's revelation; nor can we adequately treat here the theonomous argu- ment (which we thoroughly reject) that believing Christians ought to or can successfully impose biblical standards on an unwilling secular, pluralistic society. We have discussed these important issues elsewhere: see, e.g., Montgomery, *The Shaping of America*, (1976), 152 and *Human Rights and Human Dignity*, (2nd ed., 1995).

[62]   Thomas Mann, *The Tables of the Law*, (H.T. Lowe-Porter trans., 1945), 61–62.

the fall of it'. Blessed is the nation whose God is the Lord, and only those nations and individuals who seek first God's kingdom and righteousness have the spiritual wherewithal to survive the pressures of a sinful world. 'Higher law' is needed not only for sound legal decision, but for the very preservation of the legal system itself; flaunting God's law invites the simultaneous collapse of society and of the positive law that cements it together. Again, hear Thomas Mann's Moses:

> But cursed be the man who stands up and says: '[God's Commandments] are good no longer'. Cursed be he who teaches you: 'Up and be free of them, lie, steal, and slay, whore, dishonour father and mother and give them to the knife, and you shall praise my name because I proclaim freedom to you'. Cursed be he who sets up a calf and says: 'There is your God. To its honour do all this, and lead a new dance about it'. Your God will be very strong; on a golden chair will he sit and pass for the wisest because he knows the ways of the human heart are evil from youth upwards. But that will be all that he knows; and he who only knows that is as stupid as the night is black, and better it were for him had he never been born. For he knows not of the bond between God and man, which none can break, neither man nor God, for it is unviolate. Blood will flow in streams because of his black stupidity, so that the red pales from the cheek of mankind, but there is no help, for the base must be cut down. And I will lift up My foot, saith the Lord, and tread him into the mire – to the bottom of the earth will I tread the blasphemer, an hundred and twelve fathoms deep, and man and beast shall make a bend around the spot where I trod him in, and the birds of the air high in their flight shall swerve that they fly not over it. And whosoever names his name shall spit towards the four quarters of the earth, and wipe his mouth and say 'God save us all!' that the earth may be again the earth – a vale of troubles, but not a sink of iniquity. Say Amen to that!
> And
> all
> the
> people
> said
> Amen.[63]

(3) *Together with the revealed law, Scripture imparts gospel, thereby offering not only perfect standards but also merciful help for a fallen race that continually violates them.* Classical theology distinguishes three 'uses' of the law set forth in the Bible:[64] the 'political use' (law as the fundament of society, in the sense in which we have just been discussing it), the 'didactic use' (law as a guide for the spiritual growth of the believer), and the 'pedagogical use' (the law as 'schoolmaster to bring us to Christ, that we might be justified

---

[63] *Idem*, at 62–63.

[64] See J.W. Montgomery, 'The Law's Third Use', in his *The Suicide of Christian Theology*, (1970), 423.

by faith').[65] This 'pedagogical use', which Luther regarded as primary, is the law's function to show us how far short we fall, as individuals and as nations, from the perfect standard of God's will. Perhaps we have not literally violated the commandments against adultery or murder, but Jesus tells us in the Sermon on the Mount that lust and hatred are the spiritual equivalents of such acts;[66] and 'whoever shall keep the whole law, and yet offend in one point, is guilty of all'.[67] Thus 'all have sinned and come short of the glory of God'.[68] But here the gospel of God's free grace in Christ enters the picture: He came to earth for us, took our guilt on himself, died to free us from the death we deserved, and offers restoration to all who come to him in faith.[69] Luther drove this truth home in characteristically powerful words:

> This is the proper and absolute use of the law: by lightning, by tempest, and by the sound of the trumpet (as on Mount Sinai) to terrify, and by thundering to beat down and rend in pieces that beast which is called man's opinion of his own righteousness. Therefore said God by Jeremiah the prophet: 'My Word is a hammer, breaking rocks.' For as long as the opinion of his own righteousness abides in man, so long there abides also incomprehensible pride, presumption, security, hatred of God, contempt of his grace and mercy, ignorance of the promises and of Christ.[70]

Biblically revealed law thus destroys our self-image as just and righteous persons and forces us to rely on God's mercy in Christ. It gives us a true picture of ourselves, and teaches us not only justice but also mercy. Needless to say, these lessons are fundamental to the personal growth and maturity of people in general, and of members of the legal profession in particular. Without learning them, can the jurist ever pray, as all jurists should: '[N]ot a single time in rendering judgment have I forgotten that I am a poor human creature, a slave of error, that not a single time in sentencing a man has my conscience not been disturbed, trembling

---

[65]   Gal. 3:24. The Greek word translated 'schoolmaster' in the King James Version (*paedagogos*) referred not to the teacher himself but to the slave whose responsibility it was to take the pupil to the teacher.

[66]   Mt. 5:17ff.

[67]   Jas. 2:10; cf. Mt. 5:48.

[68]   Rom. 3:23.

[69]   Jn. 3:16; Rom. 5:6–8; 6:23; Eph. 2:8–9.

[70]   M. Luther, 'In Epistolam S. Pauli ad Galatas commentarius', (1531), in 40 *WA*, (the standard, critical *Weimarer Ausgabe* of the Reformer's writings), pt. 1 at 482. For an English translation of Luther's great Galatians Commentary, see P.S. Watson's rev. (1956) of the Middleton ed., (cited passage at 299); see also M. Luther, *Selections*, 141 (J. Dillenberger, ed., 1961). Cf. C.F.W. Walther, *The Proper Distinction Between Law and Gospel*, (1928), *passim*.

before an office which ultimately can belong to none but thee, O Lord'?[71]

(4) *In the face of the inadequacies and failures of even the best of human justice, biblical revelation assures us of a Last Judgment, where perfect justice shall be rendered.* The entertaining volume *'Pie-Powder', Being Dust from the Law Courts*, written anonymously by J.A. Foote, KC, contains the following anecdote:

> There stands in the market-place of one of our Wessex towns a memorial cross – not, indeed, ancient, and scarcely beautiful, but bearing an inscription which is still read at assize time with wonder and rustic awe. It tells how one Ruth Pierce, of Potterne, did in the year 1753 combine with three others to buy a sack of wheat, each contributing her share of the price. When the money was collected a deficiency appeared, and each woman protested that she had paid her full share, Ruth, in particular, declaring that if she spoke untruly she wished that God might strike her dead. Thereupon it is recorded that she instantly fell lifeless to the ground, and the money was found hidden in her right hand. The inscription adds that this signal judgment of the Almighty was commemorated by the direction of the Mayor and Aldermen for the instruction of posterity . . .
>
> . . . So have I, when passing from the market cross of Devizes to the Assize Courts hard by, reflected how much more easily justice would be administered if all perjury were cut as short as that of ill-fated Ruth.[72]

But 'ill-fated Ruth' is hardly a common phenomenon, however we explain it. 'Justice is not only to be done; it is manifestly to be done'; yet, as a matter of fact, it is often not done, manifestly or otherwise. John Chipman Gray records the viewpoint, which has occurred to all of us at one time or another, that it is 'an absurdity to say that the Law of a great nation means the opinions of half-a-dozen old gentlemen, some of them, conceivably, of very limited intelligence'.[73] Our legal systems suffer from the fallibility of the sinful human situation: absurdities are made law; guilty men go free; innocent men are punished. But Holy Scripture promises a Last Assize, when 'there is nothing covered that shall not be revealed, neither hid that shall not be known'.[74] The Judge on that Day will be at the same time omniscient and just, and the ambiguities and failures of human justice through history will be rectified. Thus the biblically revealed conception of 'higher law' offers eschatological hope: the promise that justice is not in the final analysis sound and fury, signifying

---

[71] P. Calamandrei, *Eulogy of Judges*, (1942), 101.

[72] [J.A. Foote], ' "Pie-Powder", Being Dust from the Law Courts', *Collected and Recollected on the Western Circuit by a Circuit Tramp*, (1911, reprinted 1967), 213–14.

[73] J.C. Gray, *The Nature and Sources of the Law*, (2nd ed., R. Gray, 1921, reprinted 1963), 213–14.

[74] Lk. 12:2–3.

nothing.[75] Scripture uses legal imagery to describe that Day, and stresses that the only hope for the individual or nation before the bar of eternal justice will be the services of the divine Advocate – Jesus Christ – whose death alone can free men from their sins.[76] His services are available free, through faith. Every attorney should therefore ponder, while he has the opportunity, the eternal implications of that well-known aphorism: 'The accused who acts as his own lawyer has a fool for a client.'

But, as a matter of fact, legal philosophy in modern times has very largely played the fool. In the terms of our introductory fable, it has created the conditions for its own destruction: the jurisprudential hare, by opting for moral relativity, has made himself a ready dish for the opportunist foxes of the contemporary world of *realpolitik*.

And how did this sad state of affairs come about? It has been well said that in the eighteenth century the *Bible* was killed (by unwarranted destructive criticism, as in Paine's *Age of Reason*); in the nineteenth century *God* was killed (Nietzsche's 'death of God' and the substitution of the *Uebermensch*, the Superman, who 'transvalues all values'); and in our twentieth century *Man* has been killed (in the most destructive wars in history). This degeneration is not accidental; each step logically follows from what has preceded: the loss of the Bible leads to the loss of God, for in the Bible God is most clearly revealed; the loss of God leaves Man at the naked mercy of his fellows, where might makes right.

A precisely parallel deterioration can be charted in the history of jurisprudence:

		In general	In jurisprudence
18th century}	Destruction	Bible	Revealed Law
19th century}	of	God	Natural Law
20th century}		Man	Positive Law

To the end of the Reformation period, jurisprudents grounded positive law and natural law in biblical revelation – where the clearest expression of God's revealed will for men could be found. During the eighteenth century, efforts were made by Deists and others to separate Natural Law from the Bible and to rely on 'natural rights' alone as the basis of human society and positive law.[77] But by the nineteenth century a Natural Law

---

[75]   See K. Heim, *Jesus the World's Perfecter: The Atonement and the Renewal of the World*, (1959), pt. 3; J.P. Martin, *The Last Judgment*, (1963); and especially M. Barth, *Acquittal by Resurrection*, (1964), ch. 4.

[76]   1 Jn. 2:1; Rom. 14:10–12; Phil. 2:10.

[77]   Fortunately, the American founding fathers (with the prominent exception of Jefferson) did not consciously attempt to cut themselves off from their revelational roots (see E.S. Corwin, *The 'Higher Law' Background of American Constitutional Law*, [1955]). In developing their views of 'inalienable rights' and social contract they followed not the deistic sentimentalist Rousseau but

independent of Scripture had become so vague that it was readily replaced by 'legal realism', positivism, and other relativistic approaches. Then, in our time, came the inevitable holocaust: if law is indeed relative, it can be twisted in a totalitarian, revolutionary or anarchical manner according to the desires of those in power, and become no more than a tool of the party for effecting social change according to whatever definition of social value or disvalue happens to be theirs. [78] George Orwell's *1984* appears on the horizon, as does the Antichrist of Scripture, significantly denominated 'The Lawless One'. [79]

Like Western man in general, the modern jurisprudent made the fundamental error two centuries ago of thinking that human values could be sustained apart from God's revelation of himself in Holy Scripture. An attempt was made to live off the inherited moral capital of the Bible after dispensing with it. Eventually, daddy's (Daddy's) money ran out, and the modern lawyer now finds himself in a far country 'filling his belly with the husks that the swine did eat'. [80] But – *Deo gratias!* – the lights in the Father's house are still burning, and a return to the 'higher law' of Scripture is open to all. The prodigal philosopher of law need only 'come to himself', arise and go to his Father, saying to him: 'Father, I have sinned against heaven, and before thee.' The promise is that he will be received with compassion: for this my jurisprudential son was dead, and is alive again; he was lost, and is found.

[77] *(continued)* John Locke – whose Christian orientation was such that he wrote an apologetic titled *The Reasonableness of Christianity*, (cf. C. Becker, *The Declaration of Independence: A Study in the History of Ideas* , (rev. ed., 1942). Jefferson's antipathy to Blackstone doubtless related not only to the latter's political but also to his religious conservatism; see J.S. Waterman, 'Thomas Jefferson and Blackstone's Commentaries', in D.H. Flaherty (ed.), *Essays in the History of Early American Law*, (1969), 451, 472–73.

[78] Cf. *Radical Lawyers: Their Role in the Movement and in the Courts* , (J. Black, ed., 1971).

[79] 2 Thess. 2:8.

[80] Lk. 15:16ff.

4

The Concept of Commitment in Law and Legal Science

Thomas Glyn Watkin

I. Introduction

The purpose of this examination of the concept of commitment in law and legal science is fourfold. Firstly, it will seek to identify a concept of commitment which is present in both Scripture and the tradition of the Christian church, a concept which therefore may be said to belong within a Christian legal culture. Secondly, it will seek to examine a variety of legal institutions to ascertain whether in fact such a concept is present in legal orders which are espousedly Christian or which have been shaped in societies which were or are overtly Christian. Thirdly, it will suggest that this concept can be used as a measure of determining whether a particular society is pursuing a legislative policy which carries it in a direction which furthers or hinders the spread of the gospel or indeed the kingdom of God; and, fourthly, it is hoped that in so doing a method of constructing a Christian critique of laws and legal systems will be demonstrated.

II. The Concept of Commitment Biblically and Historically

The concept of *commitment* under discussion is one which is drawn from Scripture. It is a translation of the Hebrew word *hesed*, a word which, it is widely acknowledged, is very difficult to translate into modern English. It is sometimes rendered as 'mercy', sometimes as 'loving kindness', sometimes 'loyalty', but perhaps is most accurately translated as 'stead - fastness', in particular 'steadfast love'. It has connotations of the steadfast - ness or commitment which a superior shows to an inferior, and one which does not arise out of obligation but of choice, as a result of an act of will. In that it is not a matter of obligation but of free choice, and of a choice made within a pre-existing relationship, it has been tellingly described as an act of inner faithfulness and therefore of grace.[1]

Scriptural examples undoubtedly abound.[2] Central to them all, however, is the inner faithfulness of God himself to his people, an inner faithfulness which is made manifest in his commitment to them within a covenant relationship, firstly with Noah after the flood, then with Abraham that through his seed all the nations of the earth shall be blessed, and finally in the new covenant in the blood of Christ, by which mankind and arguably the whole of creation are redeemed and restored into a right relationship with the God who is its creator and sustainer.

God's inner faithfulness, his commitment, within these successive covenant relationships is manifested in his refusal, of free choice, to regard the breach of the covenant by the other party as a cause for, in legal terms, rescission on his part.[3] Although the children of Israel depart from their allegiance, their commitment, to their God, God does not abandon them. Although they may be chastened for their disobedience, whether in the wilderness or during the Babylonian captivity, ultimately they are restored, because although they have failed in their allegiance to God, God is unfailing in his commitment, his steadfast love for them. The greatest manifestation of this commitment comes in the incarnation, death and resurrection of Christ. To restore a right relationship

---

[1]   See K.D. Sakenfeld, *Faithfulness in Action: Loyalty in Biblical Perspective*, (Philadelphia, Fortress Press, 1985); *The Meaning of* Hesed *in the Hebrew Bible*, (Harvard Semitic Monographs 17: Missoula, Montana, Scholars Press, 1973).

[2]   See, for example, the instances involving David with Jonathan and Saul's family generally: 1 Sam. 20:8, 12–17; 2 Sam. 9:1, 3, 7. For a general discussion, see B.W. Anderson, *The Living World of the Old Testament*, (4th ed., London, 1975), 308.

[3]   It has been argued that the covenant with Israel is unilateral and that therefore it was not possible for the Israelites to be in breach (see F. Lyall, 'Of Metaphors and Analogies: Legal Language and Covenant Theology' (1979), 32 *Scottish Journal of Theology*, 1–17). Although God's promise to Abraham is a unilateral obligation on God's part, nevertheless there is an agreement between them by which Abraham promises to adopt circumcision as a sign of the covenant. Uncircumcision is described by God himself as a breach of the covenant: 'the uncircumcised man child whose flesh of his foreskin is not circumcised, that soul shall be cut off from his people; he hath broken my covenant' (Gen. 17:14). However, as both promises are unilateral, the breach of one party does not absolve the other from performance, although it would be inequitable for the party in breach to seek performance from the party who had kept faith. Nevertheless, there is nothing to prevent the faithful party performing as of grace and demonstrating his steadfast commitment to the covenant. This God repeatedly does in the face of Israel's failure and defiance.

between God and man, a relationship marred by man's disobedience, God takes the initiative and becomes man in the person of Jesus Christ to pay on the cross the debt mankind owes to God, in a just settlement which once made is overtaken by divine mercy in the resurrection to eternal life.[4]

The church thereafter has manifested this commitment, this inner faithfulness, in its ministrations in the world. Most notably, and least controversially in that what follows transcends almost all divisions in the body of Christ, this commitment is manifested in baptism.[5] In baptism, the candidate asks, either personally or through the agency of sponsors or godparents, to be made an inheritor of the kingdom of God by acceptance that Christ has paid in full on his or her behalf the recompense for man's disobedience to God's will. The candidate, or his or her sponsors or godparents, makes certain promises, promises which are made in solemn form by question and answer reminiscent of the verbal contracts of ancient law, such as the Roman *stipulatio*. These give rise to unilateral obligations. The candidate amongst other things promises to renounce all sinful desires and to obediently keep God's holy will and command - ments all the days of his or her life.[6] What the candidate promises, without disrespect, could be termed a tall order. However, whether the candidate keeps the promises or not, God remains faithful to what he has promised, to the unilateral obligation into which he has entered. This is often misunderstood, and those who have fallen away from allegiance to Christ, or at least from attendance at church, sometimes ask to be rebaptised when they return to the Christian fold. This is refused for the simple reason that there is no need for God to renew his side of the bargain

---

[4]   Although theologians disagree concerning the nature of the atonement, the view expressed here is based on that given by Paul in his epistle to the Romans and developed by St Anselm in his *Cur Deus Homo*.

[5]   Baptism is classified as a dominical sacrament in many Christian traditions, dominical in that it is commanded by Christ himself: 'Go ye therefore and teach all nations, baptizing them in the name of the Father, and of the Son, and of the Holy Ghost' (Mt. 28:19); a sacrament in that it is an outward and visible sign of a grace which is inward and spiritual (this being the definition of a sacrament given in the Catechism of the Church of England's *Book of Common Prayer* of 1662). By means of the grace conferred, of which the sacrament is a sign, the candidate is said to be incorporated into the body of Christ. Where the candidate has not made the promises on his or her own behalf, some churches require them to be renewed personally at confirmation, when the candidate receives confirmation of that which was promised to him at baptism.

[6]   The questions and answers referred to here reflect the baptismal rites of the Anglican church in Wales, but the approach and content of the rite is similar in virtually every part of Christendom.

because he has never reneged on it. He has remained faithful to the obligation into which he entered.[7]

The same is true of the promises made in other rites, such as confirmation, ordination and perhaps most importantly for our purposes marriage, which some churches regard as sacraments or sacramental rites and others do not. Certainly, at ordination, the authority given to the ordinand is not dependent upon his or her faithful fulfilment of the promises made, else the consequences would indeed be dire. Although humanity fails, God does not fail and remains faithful regardless of human weakness and frailty. In marriage, however, this becomes a more complex issue. Marriage in canon law has almost always been interpreted as a consensual contract, dependant upon the consent of the parties involved, the husband and wife. Civil law, with some notable exceptions,[8] has in recent centuries insisted upon certain formalities for the consents to be valid. In addition, the formalities generally involve the making of solemn verbal promises of the question and answer type redolent again of the Roman *stipulatio* or even *sponsio*, which gave rise to unilateral obligations. Christian marriage, in addition, is said to exist not only for the procreation and upbringing of children and for the mutual help, comfort and society that the spouses ought to afford one another, but also to signify the mystical union that is betwixt Christ and his church, which again involves unilateral obligations.[9] If the promises are looked upon as a pair of unilateral obligations, each binding without reference to the other, difficult questions arise if one of the spouses breaks the promises made solemnly to the other. Can breach by one party allow the other to rescind, or should the other remain faithful to the commitment made despite the betrayal of the other, so as to manifest the steadfast love which God shows mankind, which Christ shows his church, a commitment of which the marriage relationship is meant to be a sign?[10]

---

[7]   Many churches now cater for this problem by allowing for the renewal of baptismal vows by the faithful generally as part of, for instance, the Vigil of Easter. The sacrament of reconciliation in Catholic churches also allows the penitent to confess his or her failures to live up to the promises made and receive assurance of God's steadfast love in the absolution pronounced in his name.

[8]   Scotland continues to recognise marriage by cohabitation with habit and repute, see F. Lyall, 'Marriage in Scotland', in *Marriage and Religion in Europe, Proceedings of the European Consortium on Church and State, Augsburg 1991*, (Milan, Giuffrè Editore, 1993), 1–24.

[9]   To use the language of the 1662 Anglican *Book of Common Prayer*.

[10]   Eph. 5:25–33. See also the chapter on 'The Teaching of Jesus on Marriage and Divorce' (London, 1970), in J. Duncan and M. Derrett, *Law in the New Testament*, 363–388. Marriage also poses problems for the superior–inferior dimension claimed to be essential to *hesed*.

It is easy enough against this background to discern from where the canonical concept of the indissolubility of marriage arises, although to enforce such indissolubility is to depart from a key factor in the concept of *hesed*, namely that that level of commitment must be a matter of free choice, not of obligation. Most legal systems no longer wish to enforce this view by insisting upon the indissolubility of the marriage vows, but equally they uphold the ideal, and individuals who maintain their commitment in spite of the unfaithfulness of the other party may properly be regarded as manifesting grace by their conduct. However, there can be no doubt either that those societies which continue to insist that marriage is a life-long union and not, as was the case for instance in Roman law, one which could end by the agreement of the parties or even by the repudiation of one by the other, do give witness to the Christian meaning of the relationship and to the concept of commitment which it embodies. This can indeed be maintained even if the society in question permits divorce, insofar as in a Christian society the marital obligations must ultimately be upheld by the parties' free choice and not by coercion or obligation.[11]

III. The Concept of Commitment in Action within a Legal System

How might a modern legal order manifest such commitment in its structures and purposes? First of all, it should be emphasised that what is meant here is not whether a legal order needs to be devised so as to ensure that the people who live within it or under it remain steadfastly loyal to God or the church. Rather what is meant is what signs would be expected in a legal system, what degree of commitment should be expected from the State through its laws to its citizens or subjects, in order that that State be seen to embody a reflection of the order God wills for mankind. A legal system can hardly create a state of grace in society let alone enforce one, but its provisions can encourage and be signs of inward grace in the relationships which support the social order. One would legitimately expect such signs to appear in the legal order of a Christian society.

---

[11] Thus, English law continues to present marriage as a life-long union although divorce *a vinculo matrimonio* has now been a possibility for 140 years. Scots law also upholds the life-long nature of marriage despite having countenanced divorce since the Reformation (see F. Lyall, *Of Presbyters and Kings*, (Aberdeen University Press, 1980)). Nevertheless, the resulting position stresses what marriage is regarded as being, and therefore regards unions that do not so continue as being exceptions or even failures. Many modern secular systems require attempts at reconciliation between the parties to have been made before a petition to dissolve their marriage will be entertained in the courts.

The written constitutions of many modern countries undoubtedly are attempts to express the commitment of the people, through the State, to one another. A commitment that all should enjoy, for instance, liberty, justice and security, should further be advanced by protection of basic rights such as those to life, physical integrity and freedom of movement and so on. One can scarcely doubt that if a State takes such guarantees sufficiently seriously to establish mechanisms by which citizens can challenge even legislative enactments where such are perceived to violate the fundamentally guaranteed rights, then that State is showing a very high level of commitment to its express goals and their achievement. It is worth noting that such written constitutional guarantees often first appeared in countries ruled by what are nowadays referred to as 'enlight – ened absolute rulers', monarchs who responded to the ideas of the Natural Law school of legal science by granting bills of rights to their subjects and by enacting liberal codes of laws, particularly in the area of criminal law and justice.[12]

Criminal justice brings one close to the hub of this particular issue. One of the features of the so-called enlightened codes of criminal procedure brought into effect by the absolute monarchs of the later eighteenth century was the drastic reduction in the use of the death penalty.[13] Britain experienced the same reduction in the early nineteenth century. Until such reforms, capital punishment had been the preferred penalty for a whole range of crimes and not only for homicide. The death penalty is a perfect example of a breakdown of commitment between the more powerful ruler and the less powerful subject. It marks the end of commitment, with the State responding to some breach of duty on the part of a subject or citizen by depriving the subject of the right to life and thereby for ever ending the relationship within which the duty broken played a part. Whereas it may be perfectly lawful and indeed just to deprive a wanton killer of his or her own life in measured retribution, the absence of such a just response can validly be interpreted as a sign of mercy, of continued commitment and therefore of grace within a social order which freely chooses reform and rehabilitation of the offender in preference to the infliction of the ultimate sanction, however appropriate or just that sanction may be.

Much the same argument can be applied to life imprisonment. If life actually means life then it is an ultimate giving up on the person sentenced. A legal order which mirrors the steadfast commitment of God to his people in its own arrangements can have no place for a 'lock them up and throw away the key' mentality. Spain provides a signal example

[12]   O.F. Robinson, T.D. Fergus, W.M. Gordon, *European Legal History*, (2nd ed., London, Butterworths, 1994), 242ff.

[13]   The leading example is probably that of the Grand Duchy of Tuscany, where the future Emperor Leopold II introduced in 1786 a criminal code which abrogated the death penalty altogether; see, *op. cit.* note 12 above, 246.

of Christian commitment in its penal policy. Punishment is specifically stated to be aimed at the reformation of the convict in order that he or she can be returned into society. [14] Logically, this cannot permit of life imprisonment, and for once, logic and the law keep to the same path in life. Twenty years imprisonment is as a general rule the maximum sentence that can be imposed by a Spanish criminal court. [15] Not only the death penalty but also life imprisonment is outlawed. This is in marked contrast to policies which advocate life imprisonment for persistent offending – the 'three strikes and you're out' approach. [16] It seems much closer to our Lord's response when asked by Peter on how many occasions he should forgive his brother a wrong, as many as seven times. [17] Seventy times seven is considerably more than twice, and its message of boundless commitment appears to have inspired the penal provisions of the modern Spanish state. A legal system cannot be required to follow this approach, but where one does it can properly be regarded as a sign of grace and an indication that the society in question has reached a significant stage in its corporate Christian commitment, with grace rather than strictly regulated retaliation or retribution informing its penal policies.

Spain is of course both a predominantly Roman Catholic country and one which stands in the civil law tradition. Not all Catholic countries, however, share Spain's approach to punishment, while it is true that most civil law countries do have a written constitution marking their commit - ment as states to their citizens together with mechanisms in the form of constitutional courts to enforce the State's observance of its own guar - antees. Interestingly, while the United Kingdom does not have either a written constitution or the equivalent of a constitutional court which can invalidate unconstitutional legislation, the British constitution has been and is much admired for its commitment to the rule of law. If *hesed* should ideally be based on free choice and not compulsion, arguably the United Kingdom with its internal limits on the sovereignty of Parliament as Dicey termed them is closer to the scriptural ideal. [18]

---

[14] Constitución Española, Art. 25(2).

[15] Código Penal, Art. 36. There are instances where a longer penalty can be imposed, such as seriously aggravated homicides, see Art. 139–140. Prior to the introduction of the current Código Penal in November 1995, the maximum sentence was thirty years.

[16] In the United States, this approach was indeed adopted for serious felonies in the federal Violent Crime Control and Law Enforcement Act 1994. The development of this idea in the United States has been traced in Michelle A. Saint-Germain and Robert A. Calamei, 'Three Strikes and You're In', [1996] 24 *Journal of Criminal Justice* (1), 57.

[17] Mt. 18:21, 22.

[18] See A.V. Dicey, *An Introduction to the Study of the Law of the Constitution* , (10th ed., London, Macmillan, 1967), 80f. Since this paper was delivered in

Indeed, I have argued elsewhere that the common law itself is in part founded on the concept of steadfast faithfulness and loyalty. [19] When, in the twelfth century, Henry II first attracted litigants in significant numbers into the king's courts, he did so by making available to them remedies which compelled their feudal overlords to maintain the agreements they had made with them, their tenants. Lords granted lands to their tenants in return for services, often military services. Such grants were, in effect, payment for the hire of knights to fight on the lord's or the king's behalf. In time of peace, such grants might well be for life or might even be to the tenant and his heirs, granting him an heritable estate. It would appear, however, that during the civil wars which preceded Henry II's reign, not a few lords had reneged on such arrangements and ousted such tenants in favour of stronger, fitter or younger fighting men. Henry intervened by insisting that no one was to be made to defend his tenure of land without the king's permission, and he provided remedies by which those who had been unjustly dispossessed of their land could recover it. Thus, Henry by example exhibited to his subjects his steadfast commitment to seeing that they obtained justice and security. He also created a context in which lords could be compelled to honour commitments made to their tenants by making it difficult for them to do otherwise, by creating remedies for their tenants in the royal courts.

Henry's innovations are widely credited with the creation of the common law. He described himself in the very writs which provided these remedies as 'the lord king', emphasising that he was not only the king of his subjects but also their good lord, providing them with protection and justice, not as a matter of favour or at his caprice, but steadfastly and unfailingly. [20] Undoubtedly, some of the lords who were thereafter in all probability unable to hire fighting men other than for life

---

[18]   *(continued)*   September 1997 (on the day following the devolution referendum in Scotland), bills have been placed before Parliament, of which one will introduce judicial mechanisms for determining the respective competences of the Scottish and Westminster Parliaments and another will give to the courts powers to declare that duly enacted statutes are incompatible with the European Convention on Human Rights. On the latter point, see I. Leigh, 'Towards a Christian Approach to Religious Liberty', above at p. 31, esp. 59–71.

[19]   See 'Steadfastness in the Formation of the English Common Law', a paper given at the Eleventh International Romano-Canonical Colloquium on 'Etica e diritto nella formazione dei moderni ordinamenti giuridici', Pontifical University of the Lateran, Rome, 22–25 May 1996. The proceedings will be published in 1998.

[20]   See T.G. Watkin, 'The Political Philosophy of the Lord King', in C.W. Brooks and M. Lobban, *Communities and Courts in Britain*, (London, Hambledon Press, 1997), 1–12.

or for an heritable estate felt differently; no doubt they mourned the passing of the feudal compacts by which they were able to hire knights for as long as they were able to fight and dispense with their services when they became old or infirm or unfit. One can understand that when the kingdom had been vulnerable to external attack and internal disorder, the need for an efficient fighting force demanded that the fittest knights be employed, but in time of peace under a settled government, different terms had been agreed and Henry saw good reason to uphold those obligations while peace and stability endured, for peace and stability were more likely to endure if private armies were not recruited. One can perhaps be forgiven for hearing in one's imagination the doleful voices of the disappointed nobles complaining that military tenancies were not meant to be jobs for life.

IV. The Concept of Commitment as a Critical Criterion

That no one has a job for life has become almost a refrain in statements these days with regard to employment conditions in our society. It is a refrain which is repeated as though it were some ultimate truth. It is seemingly denied that there is a choice: one can choose between building a society upon the shifting sands of insecurity of employment or, as Henry II did, choose to recognise that security of tenure for oneself or for one's family is what the vast majority of people actually want. However, there is a choice, and a Christian critique of law or of a legal system must have guidance to offer with regard to how that choice should be made.

During the years since the end of the Second World War, the Italian republic has created a career structure for the magistracy which might well be taken to be an exemplar of the commitment of a State to give its servants a job for life, almost the ultimate in job security. In Italy, as in many continental jurisdictions, the magistracy is a legal career quite distinct from that of practising as an advocate. Law graduates who wish to become judges make that career choice usually at the time of graduation. Although the examinations for entrance to the judiciary are amongst the most difficult of all the civil service examinations, successful candidates are upon admission set upon a career path which is in many ways more of an escalator, in that once they are on it, they can confidently expect to be taken to the highest salary level and status without having to compete with their peers. After a two-year period as an *uditore* or auditor – a sort of trainee judge – the young magistrate is promoted, almost automatically, to the status and salary of a judge of first instance, a judge of the *Tribunale*. This promotion, like all others in the Italian magistracy, is freely given provided that there are no black marks against the candidate. In other words, promotion is only obstructed in the case of demerit; there is no competition on the basis of merit. Again, after eleven years at the level of a judge of *Tribunale*, the magistrate is promoted for the asking, provided there is no demerit against him, to the status and salary of a judge of the Appeal Court. Seven years further service at that status entitles the judge to promotion to the level of a judge of the Supreme Court of *Cassazione*, and after a further eight years at that level, there is again promotion, subject only to the absence of negative factors, to the status and salary of an office superior, that is a judge who is qualified to be the head of a particular judicial area or court. These promotions, and the salary increases which go with them, are not dependent upon there being vacancies among the judges of the courts of the level concerned. Nor do they require, indeed there is no expectation, that the promoted magistrate will move to the new level for which he or she is qualified. The system is grounded on the belief that only by freeing the judiciary from competitive pressures and temptations to please the powers that be can efficient and impartial administration of justice be guaranteed. In Italy, as the events of the early 1990s demonstrate, the judiciary has achieved a remarkable degree of independence from political control, and has indeed been able to attempt at any rate to cleanse the Augean stables of the Italian political system. Whether such influence, or perhaps even power, is a good thing is not the question of present concern. What is clear is that the career structure of the magistracy in Italy exhibits a commitment by the State to its judges which frees them to perform their function from initial qualification to retirement. [21]

Quite simply, what the Italian magistrates enjoy is security of tenure. They are given, if not a life interest in their job, at least an interest which is guaranteed for their working lives. A proper comparison can be made with what Henry II achieved during his reign for military tenants, who were no longer to hold land at the will of their lords but for life or even heritably. Such security of tenure can be identified in a variety of occupations and professions until relatively recent times. It is still a feature, for instance, of the terms upon which the cure of souls of a parish in the Church of England is entrusted to an incumbent. In that context, the tenure of the incumbent is referred to as the parson's freehold.

It is worth reflecting for a moment on what granting a cleric such security of tenure means in the context of his relationship with the ecclesiastical authorities. It is in effect a clear commitment to the

---

[21] See T.G. Watkin, *The Italian Legal Tradition*, (Aldershot, Ashgate, 1997), 115–121; 'Seeds of Revolution', (1994), 144 *New Law Journal*, 431. It should be emphasised that the Italian system does not entail any loss of expectation that a magistrate will increase in efficiency and judgement as his or her career progresses. Such improvement is part and parcel of there being no demerit. Failure to develop one's capability could be a demerit, but where such development is achieved, the due reward must follow regardless of whether others have done better or the individual in question might have done even more.

incumbent as an individual. It is a recognition that having satisfied the bishop who grants him the cure of souls, a cure which is, in the bishop's words of institution, both thine and mine, the benefice is entrusted to him thereafter. Once deemed fit to receive the living, the cleric cannot thereafter be removed other than for most serious cause. Provided that he is not guilty of serious doctrinal or moral impropriety, the cleric is virtually immovable. It is a commitment to trust him to minister to the needs of the parish, to preach the gospel and minister the sacraments, according to his judgement. He cannot be moved on because he offends the people by his preaching, perhaps by challenging their response. Nor can he be moved on for failing to respond to what might be termed the requirements of line-management within the church. He cannot be removed by his ecclesiastical superiors for anything other than a serious breach of discipline, and as is nowadays widely appreciated, the proce - dures of the ecclesiastical courts make such deprivations and depositions very difficult to achieve. In short, the Church of England has tradition - ally shown an almost total commitment to its parochial clergy, a commitment which it can well be argued mirrors the covenant com - mitment of God to his people and of Christ to his church. In the ecclesiastical setting, such a manifestation of commitment, however at times inconvenient and even prejudicial to the popular view of what benefits the church, is entirely fitting and indeed quasi-sacramental in its significance.[22]

This is not intended to suggest that all churches should adopt these arrangements. What is suggested is that within the hierarchical framework of the Church of England, there exist structures which can manifest divine grace in the commitment of the bishop, as chief pastor of his diocese, to the individual parish priests who receive the cure of souls in their several benefices at his hands. According to this structure, the individual minister is responsible to the bishop, who as chief pastor of the diocese is responsible for the welfare of the flock therein, and not to the local congregation itself. In churches where the minister is accountable to the local congregation, a different relationship exists which, lacking the superior-to-inferior dimension of the Anglican arrangement, will not manifest the grace of commitment in the same manner. Opportunity for commitment, perhaps with a greater degree of free choice, will exist. The structure of the Anglican arrangement, however, gives its churches a particular opportunity to show forth commitment in their corporate life.

Such tenure has not been confined to ecclesiastical persons. In the universities also, partly in imitation of the church's arrangements, tenure

---

[22] Quasi-sacramental in that it is an outward sign of inner faithfulness, as a sacrament is an outward and visible sign of an inner and spiritual grace (see n. 5 above), and an act of inner faithfulness which constitutes *hesed* is said to be evidence of grace.

has been a feature of academic appointments.[23] After a brief probationary period of three or perhaps five years, an academic in the United Kingdom could expect until quite recently to enjoy security of employment until retiring age.[24] The reasons for granting academics such security were not that different from those which pertained to the clergy; an academic was thereby liberated to speak his or her mind without fear or favour. To disagree with a prevailing orthodoxy, to present opinions which might seem eccentric in their difference, could not ground a case for dismissal. As with the clergy, serious misconduct alone could lead to an academic being deprived of his post, and the processes by which that could be achieved were shrouded in some uncertainty. Academic tenure was in a very real sense the legal basis of academic freedom, and marked the commitment of the university or other institution to the individual it had employed. This commitment was one which it would honour, as superior to inferior, almost regardless of what the individual did or did not do, provided the essential duties of the post were not neglected. That commitment might not always be rewarded, but certainly it manifested a loyalty that did not depend on rapid results or the shifting demands of successive governments in terms of research assessments or other short-term criteria. It manifested a belief rather that the individual who had been entrusted with an academic post deserved the commitment of his employers throughout his working life, provided only that he continued to perform his duties conscientiously.

For a short period in the last few decades, it appeared that such job security, based on a steadfast commitment between employer and em-ployee, was fated to spread into other areas of work. Legislation protecting

---

[23]   This was not always the case in the universities, where quite mercenary contractual arrangements were often previously the norm. A notorious example concerns the great Renaissance jurist, Andrea Alciati, in his relations with the law faculty at Avignon. Having been hired in 1518 at a stipend of 300 ducats, he prudently left Avignon in 1521 when the university was closed owing to an outbreak of plague. He returned in November of that year when the university reopened, but the plague again appeared in 1522 when the university again had to be closed. At this time, Alciati's contract came up for renewal and the university offered renewal subject to the stipend ceasing to be payable if the university was forced to close. Alciati refused these terms, which although they appear somewhat pusillanimous, took account of the fact that Alciati had resumed practice in Italy during the periods of closure. For further details, see Coleman Phillipson, 'Andrea Alciati and his Predecessors', in Sir John Macdonell and Edward Manson (ed.), *Great Jurists of the World*, (Boston, Little Brown & Co., 1914; reprinted New York, Rothman Reprints, 1968), 58ff.

[24]   Tenure in British universities was removed by the provisions of the Education Reform Act 1988, ss. 203, 204. More generally, see ss. 202–208 of the Act.

employees from unfair dismissal, together with tribunals to enforce their rights, appeared upon the United Kingdom legal scene.[25] However, in many respects, the clock, if not the calendar, has since been turned back. In the face of greater protection of employees from unfair dismissal, employers have tended more and more to favour fixed-term contracts, and even in the Church of England there has been an increasing tendency for bishops to appoint priests-in-charge to parishes in preference to incumbents, thus denying them the freehold and making them removable at will, thereby forfeiting a clear opportunity to manifest commitment within a hierarchical relationship. In some areas therefore, clergy of the established church have ended up with the worst of both worlds – no longer having the protection of the freehold but still being classed as self-employed and not as employees, thus rendering them outside the protection of the unfair dismissal laws.[26] In the universities, much the same is true. Instead of showing a clear commitment and confidence in staff when recruited, it is now increasingly rare for a university to give a permanent post to an academic under thirty. While young, aspiring academics are expected to show great loyalty, productivity, efficiency, in short commitment, to their employer, very little commitment is shown in return, and financial pressures more than merit may dictate whether a contract will be renewed. It is a situation which reverses the *hesed* ideal of the, in this case, economically stronger party showing inner faithfulness and steadfast commitment to the weaker party. Those wanting permanent posts are regularly required to jump through all manner of hoops in the hope of being favoured but with no guarantees. It is a radical change from the tenurial concept of university employment, and one which deserves a careful critique from the perspective of Christian values in our social and economic arrangements.

This is not to say that financial difficulties should not affect employment prospects, including the prospects of continued employment. There is

---

[25] Legislation regarding unfair dismissal can be found for instance in the Industrial Relations Act 1971, ss. 22–32; the Trade Union and Labour Relations Act 1974, ss. 22–24; the Employment Protection (Consolidation) Act 1978, s. 54. The provisions of the last-mentioned statute are now contained in section 94 of the Employment Rights Act 1996 which states that: 'An employee has the right not to be unfairly dismissed by his employer'. Procedures to adjudicate concerning unfair dismissals are provided by ss. 111–132 of the 1996 Act, together with Part I, particularly ss. 7, 10, 13 and 18 of the Industrial Tribunals Act 1996.

[26] A position recently reaffirmed in *Southwark Diocese* v *Coker*, [1996] Industrial Cases Reports (ICR) 896 (affirming *Davies* v *Presbyterian Church of Wales*, [1986] 1 All ER 705, and reversing *Coker* v *Southwark Diocese*, [1995] ICR 563), a decision upheld by the Court of Appeal in *Diocese of Southwark* v *Coker*, [1998] ICR 140.

no virtue in letting an enterprise fall into bankruptcy and having to dispense with the services of all the employees if reducing the workforce could save the concern. What cannot, according to the view presented here, be justified is reducing the size of a workforce to increase profit - ability, where commitment to the profits of the owners, be they indi - viduals or shareholders, completely outweighs considerations of commitment to the employees. This is particularly true where the cost of benefits to the dismissed employees and their families falls upon the community, so that any increased profits are in fact subsidised by the tax-paying population at large.

Moreover, the costs to the wider public of such practices are not restricted to the financial. It is also worth contemplating where such lack of commitment in employment leads in society generally. Insecurity almost certainly breeds insecurity. It is not only in universities that young professionals are denied the sort of job security that their seniors took for granted only fifteen to twenty years ago. Increasingly, fixed-term con - tracts are the fate of the under-thirties. Without the security of permanent employment, it is increasingly difficult for young adults to enter into other kinds of commitment: difficult to commit themselves to purchasing houses; difficult to commit themselves to relationships of any degree of permanence, let alone one as permanent as marriage. It is pointless contemplating the question of why commitment within marriage or to marriage as an institution is less strong than in previous generations if one is not prepared to take on board the underlying erosion of commitment in other spheres which has removed some of the social underpinning which makes such personal commitments feasible.

One must also add to this the insecurity which those who have so-called permanent employment may feel if there is a constant threat of redundancy or redeployment. Knowledge that one's employment is only safe until the next change in company policy is hardly consonant with a feeling of inner security and peace of mind. Increasingly, there is a fair deal of competition to remain in employment, employment being almost at the pleasure of the employer, who dominates as an absolute ruler rather than governing as a faithful lord. Add to this the problems of the young unemployed who, being shown little if any commitment by the State or anyone else, do not even have the wherewithal to enjoy their lack of commitment and who are unable to show, or see no purpose in showing, commitment either to their partners or to their progeny. Again, one can hardly complain of, let alone condemn, this lack of commitment while remaining silent on lack of commitment in the social, economic and legal arrangements which increase the likelihood of such an outcome.

What is particularly ironic is that, for once, what has been undone in recent years can probably be restored in less time than it was destroyed. It is a temple that can be rebuilt in a short time. Steadfast commitment is a concept which needs to be restored to its rightful place in our society not merely that it may be Christian, but that it can be just, peaceful and secure. For what an historical precedent is worth, Henry II achieved it in less than a generation.

It might be felt that the view of steadfastness given here in relation to employment is one-sided and ignores the reciprocal duties of the em - ployee to the employer or the Christian duty to work and earn one's living. However, the biblical concept of steadfastness exists within a superior–inferior relationship not as of right but of grace, and the superior practises it without expectation of any return. It in no way contradicts the duty of the employee to work for his living or to fulfil his contractual obligations to his employer. What it does however rule out is the employer disposing of the services of his employee because it maximises or increases his profit to do so, or deliberately structuring the terms of employment so as to encourage competition amongst the workforce which will reward not those who have laboured according to their talents, but only those who have produced most or performed best. While it would be wrong to reward those who have not used the talents given them,[27] it is equally wrong not to reward the labourer for the work he has accomplished.[28] The relationship of employer and employee has its reciprocal obligations, but is also a context in which the stronger party can practise and exhibit the qualities of steadfastness which manifest the Christian ideal. The critique offered here is of a tendency in recent decades to construct work contexts which deny the opportunity to practise steadfastness and indeed appear to celebrate the virtues of inconstancy and uncertainty as means of achieving 'efficiency'. Thus, the career structure of the Italian magistracy, the tenure of clergy in the Church of England and the tenure once accorded to academic staff in the universities, all allow for removal for serious failure to perform one's duties, but do not admit of removal for the convenience of management, insisting upon commitment as long as the duties are performed faithfully. As long as one is utilising one's talents properly, the stronger party ought not to renege upon his commitment to the weaker. It has been interesting to note how the disasters which have befallen certain businesses in the Far East, which have traditionally been wedded to the concept of giving a job for life, have been greeted in the West as establishing that the market has overcome that idea. It is profitable in a non-financial sense to reflect upon which of these approaches belongs to God and which to mammon.

V. Conclusion

This paper has attempted to demonstrate that steadfast commitment is a concept which can be recognised as Christian in the sense that it is both scriptural and part of the tradition of the Christian church. Moreover, it

[27] Mt. 25:14–40.
[28] Lk. 10:7.

is clear that it has affected the development of legal institutions in many societies, in part by direct Christian influence, through the work of Christian governors, and in part indirectly through the influence of Christian teaching upon even secular theories of natural law which have in turn influenced the content and approach of many modern constitu-tions. Further, I would submit that recent and contemporary trends in our own land show the importance of the concept to social living, and that Christian lawyers have a part to play not only in offering a critique of legal developments in terms of the concept but also in action, in ensuring that where they have influence or even power, in the law firms and law schools of the land, steadfast commitment is practised as well as preached, if necessary in the teeth of institutional criticism and opposition.

While enforced commitment is hardly a sign of grace, there is nothing to prevent societies arranging the legal structures which support relation-ships within them, whether between State and citizen or employer and employee, in a manner which expects and facilitates, rather than frustrates or even derides, the practice of commitment. The normative legal view of marriage is an example of such a supportive legal structure. While it cannot be appropriate to apply the high standards of God's grace to the secular legal conditions of a fallen world, it is surely proper to expect signs of that grace operating in and through the legal arrangements of societies which comprise men and women who acknowledge the redemption of the world by his Son and who seek to live in the power of his enabling Spirit.

Finally, the paper has I hope throughout exhibited its final aim, namely a method of achieving a Christian critique of law and legal systems. There are many other concepts which can be identified as having a place in a Christian legal order or culture, and of which the presence or absence, or increase or decrease, provides a barometer for the spiritual health of the system or even of a legal theory.[29]

---

[29]   The author wishes to thank the Editor, Professor Paul Beaumont, and Mrs Teresa Sutton for their comments on an earlier draft of this chapter, as well as those who asked questions and raised points for discussion after its delivery as a paper at the Bristol conference in September 1997.

5

A Christian Approach to International Laws of Armed Conflict

H. McCoubrey

I. Introduction

The problems of war and armed conflict[1] in the modern world raise questions in Christian understanding which are by no means so easily resolved as proponents of the various possible viewpoints commonly assert. In the present context two major issues arise – one is the Christian attitude to the occurrence of war and the second is that of the Christian response to the conduct of military hostilities when in fact they do occur. The distinction between these two questions is symbolised in public international law by the division between the *jus ad bellum* and the *jus in bello*, the former dealing with resort to armed force in the conduct of international relations and the latter with constraints upon the conduct of warfare. The question of resort to armed force forms the inevitable background to discussion of limitation upon the conduct of warfare and therefore demands at least preliminary consideration.

The difficulty which besets discussion of this matter is illustrated by the very fact of a diverse, and to some extent incompatible, range of possible opinions within Christian traditions. Jesus' recorded teaching in the Christian gospel does not refer directly to questions of war, nor is there even much indirect military reference. Some such reference can be found in the Pauline epistles and in the book of Revelation,[2] but even here the reference is to spiritual struggle rather than international, or even non-international, armed conflict. At least two broad reasons may be suggested for this absence of military reference in Jesus' teaching. In the

---

[1] The term 'armed conflict' is now generally preferred because of the technicality of interpretation which has come to surround the term 'war' for certain purposes, see *Kawasaki Kisen Kabushiki Kaisha v Bantham SS Co.*, [1939] 2 KB 544.

[2] See, e.g., Eph. 6:13–17 and Rev. 9:14–17.

first place there is the supposed change from an Old Testament emphasis on the 'corporate' salvation of the people of Israel as a whole to a New Testament emphasis upon individual salvation. This supposed change of emphasis is a considerable oversimplification – the Old Testament certainly does not ignore questions of individual salvation. To take a 'quasi-military' instance, one may cite the condemnation of David's procuring the death of Uriah the Hittite in battle.[3] By the same token, the New Testament even in its 'individualistic' emphasis frequently addresses issues of individual conduct in its social context. Examples may be seen, amongst many others, in the story of Dives and Lazarus[4] and, for the present purpose very much to the point, in the parable of the good Samaritan.[5]

A second, and possibly more direct, factor can be found in Jesus' desire as one proclaiming a kingdom not of this world to defuse any expectation that he might play the role of nationalist resistance leader against the Roman occupation of Palestine. For both of these reasons, and possibly for others also, Christian teaching is without direct reference to secular war and its problems, with the result that Christian doctrine upon this subject is necessarily developed by analogy. This in turn admits a diversity of opinion which includes, by way of crude categorisation, ideas of pacifism, just war and holy war. Of these three the last may immediately be dismissed as devoid of foundation in any recognisably Christian teaching. It found its most potent expression in the medieval Crusades.[6] They originated in an appeal by Pope Urban II at the Council of Clermont in 1095 for a military campaign for the recapture of Jerusalem and the holy places from the Saracens. The First Crusade succeeded in this endeavour in 1099 and set up the short-lived Latin Kingdom of Jerusalem. The motivations for the Crusades were, however, very mixed and in many cases highly questionable. They included a strong desire to eliminate Saracen intermediaries in the profitable eastern spice trade. As Philippe Contamine comments,

---

[3] The account of David's contriving the death of Uriah the Hittite, set out in 2 Sam. 11:6–27 and 12:1–14, is clearly concerned with David as an erring individual rather than as a representative of an erring community.

[4] Lk. 16:19–31.

[5] Lk. 10:25–37. See, e.g., E.P. Saunders, *Jesus and Judaism*, (SCM, 1985).

[6] For consideration of the Crusades in the context of the Laws of War see J. Pictet, *Development and Principles of International Humanitarian Law*, (Martinus Nijhoff, 1985), 16–18. For general histories see S. Runciman, *A History of the Crusades*, 3 Vols., (Cambridge, 1951–4); J. Riley-Smith, *The Oxford Illustrated History of the Crusades*, (Oxford, 1995). There are some Old Testament passages which reflect something of the idea of a Holy War (see Deut. 20; Num. 31:7–19 and 1 Sam. 15), but these must now be read in the light of New Testament teaching on the need to love our enemies (see n. 9–13 and 70 below).

The true political objectives of Urban II are unknown. Did he simply wish to ensure the safety of the route to the Holy places . . . or to recapture for the Papacy's profit the land of Israel which he knew had once been part of the Roman Empire? . . . [T]here were leaders who had avowedly temporal ambitions . . . [o]n the other hand, the *milites* of many regions in the west responded to . . . preaching with . . . eagerness . . .[7]

The cynicism and brutality of the Crusades did much to discredit the idea of 'holy war' in Christian thinking. It is noteworthy that in the thirteenth century St Thomas Aquinas appears to have ruled out difference of religion as such as a cause of war. In *Summa Theologica* he wrote that,

> Christ's faithful often wage war with unbelievers, not indeed for the purpose of forcing them to believe, because even if they were to conquer them, and take them prisoners, they should still leave them free to believe, if they will, but in order to prevent them from hindering the faith of Christ.[8]

The idea of 'hindrance' in this context is, sadly, open to some latitude of interpretation and in practice confessional differences have continued to be a source of war. Conflict of religion played a clear role in the seventeenth-century disaster of the Thirty Years War and even at the end of the twentieth century it may be seen as an element in the conflict(s) in former Yugoslavia and in the situation in Northern Ireland.

Ideas of pacifism and just war require rather more detailed analysis. For many commentators it is taken to be obvious that pacifism is the mainstream Christian position upon war and even the only possible position. The claim of pacifism in Christian thinking is undeniably very strong, but it is not necessarily the case that support of military action is therefore ruled out for Christians in all cases. The *prima facie* case for a position of absolute pacifism nonetheless demands careful consideration.

II. The Argument of Christian Pacifism

Jesus gave us two fundamental commandments which are set out as follows in the gospel according to Mark 12:30–31,[9] 'you shall love the Lord your God with all your heart and with all your soul, and with all your mind, and with all your strength . . . You shall love your neighbour as yourself. There is no commandment greater than these.' It is clear that the fundamental command to love neighbours includes also enemies. In

---

[7] P. Contamine, trans. M. Jones, *War in the Middle Ages*, (Basil Blackwell, 1984; first published as *La Guerre au Moyen Age* by Presses Universitaires de France, 1980), 60–61.

[8] St Thomas Aquinas, *Summa Theologica*, 2a2ae 10.8 in the Dominican translation (Sheed & Ward, 1981), Vol. III, at 1213.

[9] See also Mt. 22:27–39 and Lk. 10:27.

the gospel according to Matthew it is written, 'Love your enemies and pray for those who persecute you . . . For if you love those who love you . . . And if you salute only your brethren, what more are you doing than others?'[10]

Jesus also commanded in the gospel according to Matthew, 'Do not resist one who is evil. But if anyone strikes you on the right cheek, turn to him the other also . . . and if anyone forces you to go one mile, go with him two miles.'[11] This is also stated in Luke 6:29–31, but omitting the reference to going the other mile and adding, 'as you wish that men would do to you, do so to them.'[12]

The message of love of enemies is repeated and elaborated by Paul in the epistle to the Romans 12:14, 18–19, in the exhortation to 'Bless those who persecute you: bless and do not curse them . . . If possible, so far as it depends upon you, live peaceably with all. Beloved, never avenge yourselves, but leave it to the wrath of God . . .' This Romans text is generally held to be older in its recorded written form than the gospel text as it is preserved by Matthew[13] and thus affirms the preservation of Jesus' original teaching here.

The closest approach to a direct reference to quasi-military force in the gospels, Christ's rebuke to Peter for his attack upon Malchus, the slave of the High Priest, in the Garden of Gethsemane when the Romans and the servants of the High Priest came to arrest Jesus, has become a key text in the argument of Christian pacifism. Jesus stated unequivocally that 'all who take the sword will perish by the sword.'[14] This text was taken by Tertullian in his *Treatise upon Idolatry* to have disarmed all soldiers. In this context it must however be borne in mind, as Helgeland, Daly and Patout Burns point out, that Tertullian was very much concerned in this treatise with the perils of the imperial cult which was much emphasised by the pagan Roman Empire and made involvement with it by Christians impossible, upon this if no other grounds.[15] The rebuke at Gethsemane needs, however, to be treated with some care. The arrest at Gethsemane was an unavoidable prerequisite for the passion of our Lord, an event which he could have avoided had he so chosen but which, as he accepted in his agonised debate that night, was necessary for the fulfilment of his salvific mission. A rather different question may arise if the trauma is to be inflicted upon someone else. Jesus allowed himself to be led to the cross, he did not facilitate the leading of others there – quite the contrary!

10   Mt. 5:44, 46–7.
11   Mt. 5:39,41.
12   Lk. 6:31.
13   See the *New Jerome Biblical Commentary* (Chapman/Cassell, 1990), 631 & 830.
14   Mt. 26:52.
15   J. Helgeland, R.J. Daly and J. Patout Burns, *Christianity and the Military: The Early Experience*, (SCM, 1987), 23.

The application of Jesus' love command to enemies and the condem -
nation of the use of force at Gethsemane nonetheless, at the very least,
severely restrains resort to armed force and absolutely condemns the
aggressive use of force. What then of *defensive* force where unconscionable
aggression is being, or has been, perpetrated? The preliminary point must
be made that any discussion of this subject in the English language
immediately faces a problem of limited terminology. One word, 'love',
is supposed to cover a vast range of human emotions, ranging from the
close bonding of spouses to the general affection of friends and, in a
decadent modern culture, is sadly all too often taken to be coterminous
with sexual lust. This same word is used also to express the supernatural
love of God for each and every one of his people. No single word can
carry such a burden of diverse meanings adequately. [16] In Christian
tradition the Greek word *agape* has been adopted as signifying the love
taught by Jesus. Even here, however, the concept covers a broad range
of situations and responses. In the context of warfare, and of 'enemies'
more generally, these linguistic limitations, certainly in English and to
some degree even in Greek, can make discussion seem stilted and artificial.
This is, however, more an appearance than a reality. If the later linguistic
philosophy of Wittgenstein is followed, advancing a 'games' model in
place of his earlier model of 'logical atomism', [17] the problem is much
reduced in so far as multiple usages and 'meanings' in varying contexts
allows a much broader understanding of the scope of 'love' in its various
forms than might sometimes appear to be suggested. Quite clearly the
love which exists, e.g., between spouses, will differ from that which may
be experienced between 'enemies', military or personal. The common
element of, at a bare minimum, genuine and positive concern for other
individuals and / or groups is, however, to be taken as underlying all the
many forms of love. Above all the quality of the love of God, the
overarching nature of which is stated simply by Paul in commenting that
'Christ Jesus came into the World to save sinners', [18] has a special resonance
in the present context which cannot safely be ignored. Where, then,
Christian people, meaning a society of such people, are faced with
external military aggression or witness such a threat to other people, it is
clear that the response to both the victims and the perpetrators must have
the character of love. To the fundamental question 'am I my brother's
[or sister's] keeper' [19] the answer, in war as in any other situation, is clearly
'yes'. Just how that love should be expressed in such a situation is,
however, by no means so clear, and refusal to resist the wrongdoing of

---

[16] For discussion of this see C.S. Lewis, *The Four Loves*, (London, Bles, 1960).

[17] See in particular *Philosophical Investigations*, (Blackwell, 1953) and *Philosophis-
che Grammatik*, (Blackwell, 1969). A useful discussion will be found in
A. Kenny, *Wittgenstein*, (Penguin, 1973), ch. 9.

[18] 1 Tim. 1:15.

[19] Gen. 4:9.

a brother or sister is not necessarily an act of love – either to the erring sibling or to third parties. The point is well put by Ronald Preston in his remark that,

> Briefly, love of neighbour means being responsible for our fellow human beings, not because of their idiosyncratic qualities but because of their humanity as made in the image of God . . . It does not depend on natural affection in the one who loves nor natural attractiveness in the one loved . . . [i]t does not mean submission to being exploited: for one thing it would not be for the good of the neighbour to be allowed to exploit you.[20]

The expression of love to enemies, personal or public, is not a simple matter, nor does it necessarily involve acquiescence in oppression by an enemy. Nor, of course, does it by any means necessarily call forth or justify a forceful response upon the part of oneself or one's society.

The classic, and entirely appropriate, response of Christian pacifism to a military threat is resort to prayer and this, unsurprisingly, has early origins. The argument can be found in Origen and of this J.W. Trigg remarks that,

> Origen . . . clearly taught that Jesus' prohibition of violence ruled out service in the army. . . . But Origen . . . admitted that hopes of universal peace probably could not be fulfilled on this earth. . . . Origen thus did not altogether rule out war. He recognised the legitimacy of wars for the defence of the empire. But Christians, he maintained, should not fight in those wars. . . . By destroying by their prayers the daemons who stir up strife, they serve the empire more effectively than they could with arms in their hands.[21]

This contention is also found in some Christian analyses of the Second World War.[22] The basic argument is clearly set out in C.E. Raven's comment that,

> . . . the heart of the Christian gospel is not safety but victory – the victory over evil that was won by the way of the cross. Jesus . . . chose to meet evil unarmed and unafraid to let it do its worst with him, and to bear its wounds in his own body on the tree. So by death came life . . .[23]

John Riches draws out the implications of this view, undeniable in relation to Christ's own ministry, in urging that,

> I think that we need to challenge arguments which suggest that love of enemies is either impossible or unrealistic. Even in Jesus' day, as stories in

---

20 R. Preston, 'Christian Ethics', in P. Singer, ed., *A Companion to Ethics*, (Blackwell, 1993), 91 at 98.

21 J.W. Trigg, *Origen*, (SCM, 1983), 235–6.

22 See below.

23 C.E. Raven, 'The Theological Basis of Christian Pacifism', (Fellowship of Reconciliation, 1952), cited by R. Gill in *A Textbook of Christian Ethics*, (T. & T. Clark, 1985), at 367.

Josephus make clear, non-violent resistance was not by any means ineffective. Today this may be all the more true. For in past ages it was possible to resolve international rivalries and conflicts by military engagement, by the use of coercive force, it is now in the last resort no longer so possible.[24]

It is true that some commentators, especially but not only in the USA, have suggested links between the possibility of nuclear war and the battle of Armageddon. Such ideas are most prominent in the thinking of so-called 'nuclear dispensationalism',[25] however, the attempt to make this link seems theologically and politically naive and not a little dangerous. [26] A nuclear war, it may be suggested, would be an act of supreme human folly, and sin, rather than a fulfilment of the divine purpose. The possession of nuclear weapons and the potential for their use raise many sensitive issues of theology, ethics, law, politics and strategic studies, [27] but a linkage of these weapons with the apocalypse in the former context of 'cold war' politics would have opened the door to a return to the most perverse manifestations of so-called 'holy war' thinking, in which the gospel of love is perverted into a pretext for aggressive militarism. [28]

Returning to the more general argument, it may be suggested that in its proper context Riches' argument is beyond criticism, but it is, none - theless, not the only possible position upon armed force in general. This leads to the historic Christian argument upon 'just war', although this is not in itself the foundation of the position which is here to be outlined.

III. The Use and Abuse of 'Just War' Thought in Christian Traditions

'Just war' thinking has come to have a bad reputation in the light of its historic abuse as, in effect, a 'warmongers' charter'. This abuse is unde - niable, but the doctrine itself originated as a means for the aversion of

---

[24]   J. Riches, 'The Uses of the Bible in the Nuclear Debate', in R. Bauckham and R.J. Elford (eds.), *The Nuclear Weapons Debate: Theological and Ethical Issues*, (SCM, 1989), 47 at 63.

[25]   For discussion of this see R. Bauckham, 'Facing the Future: The Challenge to Secular and Theological Presuppositions', in R. Bauckham and R.J. Elford (eds.), *The Nuclear Weapons Debate: Theological and Ethical Issues*, (SCM, 1989), 29 especially at 39–42.

[26]   See S. Maimela, 'A Theological View from the Non-Nuclear World', in *ibid.*, 16–28.

[27]   Amongst many others see R. Bauckham and R.J. Elford, *op. cit.* n. 24; R. Harris, 'The Morality of Nuclear Deterrence', in R. Harris, ed., *What Hope in an Armed World?* (Pickering, 1982), 87–114; L. Freedman, *The Evolution of Nuclear Strategy*, (Macmillan, 1981).

[28]   See above.

war and resort to military force in international relations. It emerged in its Christian forms from scholastic thought with early expression in the work of St Augustine of Hippo (345–430) and in a more developed form in the thirteenth century. St Augustine's thinking upon this subject derived from his general perception of social order as a Christian Platonist. His analysis of war was in many ways an extrapolation of his more general view of positive law. He saw positive law as defined by sin and functioning only as a necessary means of coercive correction in a fallen order within which it had its only relevance.[29] Just war was perceived as playing a similar role in 'international relations'[30] in a sinful world order – it might sometimes be necessary but is always to be regretted. It is important to note here that for St Augustine war is always conditioned by sin. As Paul Ramsay remarks, 'It is a lively sense of man's common plight in wrongdoing and of the judgment of God that overarches the justified war [in St Augustine's view], and not . . . a sense of clarity about the universal ethical standards that are to be applied.'[31] St Augustine remarked in *Contra Faustem* that a just war is one which seeks to address a gross wrong done to a State, punish a wrongdoing State or recovering a legitimate entitle - ment of the aggrieved State.[32] War is thus presented as a desperate last resort which is conceivable only in a situation inherently characterised by sin. However, the actual specification of a 'just' *causus belli* is minimal and this leaves a dangerous latitude of interpretation, especially when the essential anti-war substance of Augustinian doctrine was forgotten.

In its more elaborate thirteenth-century formulations, the essential foundation of medieval *bellum justum* thought is usefully summarised by Philippe Contamine thus,

> [T]he given classical criteria for a just war were formulated under the rubrics *persona, res, causa, animus* and *auctoritas*. Defined by Laurentius Hispanus around 1210, they were repeated almost without variation by Johannes Teutonicus, while St Raymond of Penaforte (c.1180–1275) ensured their ultimate diffusion.[33]

St Thomas Aquinas set out his thought upon war in *Summa Theologica* 2a2ae.40 and for him as for St Augustine, there is some linkage between ideas of law and theories of war. For Aquinas, just war can only be waged

[29]   For discussion of this see H. McCoubrey, *The Obligation to Obey in Legal Theory*, (Dartmouth, 1997), ch. 3.

[30]   The term is used with due allowance for difference in cultural and political context.

[31]   P. Ramsay, 'Just War according to St Augustine', in J.B. Elshtain (ed.), *Just War Theory*, (Blackwell, 1992), 8 at 16.

[32]   St Augustine of Hippo, *Contra Faustem*, LXXXIII; *Super Josue*, Qu. 10. The text is cited with approval by St Thomas Aquinas in *Summa Theologica*, 2a2ae.40,1.

[33]   P. Contamine, trans. M. Jones, *op. cit.*, 282.

by a sovereign ruler and in so doing such a person or entity will be bound to act within a defined ethical framework. In the translation offered by J.G. Dawson in A.P. d'Entreves' edition of Aquinas' political writings, the relevant section is rendered as follows,

> . . . [I]t can happen that even when war is declared by legitimate authority and there is just cause, it is, nevertheless, made unjust through evil intention. St Augustine says in *Contra Faustem* (LXXIV): 'The desire to hurt, the cruelty of vendetta, the stern and implacable spirit, arrogance in victory, the thirst for power, and all that is similar, all these are justly condemned in war.'[34]

All this said, although scholastic *bellum justum* thinking condemned war as an abomination, even if sometimes the lesser of two evils, it had in practice two radical defects. Within its own terms of reference its implementation was being corrupted and debased even whilst it was being formulated, essentially by the lack of objective modes of determining the 'justice' of participation by a State in a given armed conflict.

The second great defect of scholastic *bellum justum* theory related to the *jus in bello*. St Augustine of Hippo, St Thomas Aquinas and others all cautioned against the excessive and cruel pursuit of a cause which would render 'unjust' a cause which might have been 'just' in its origins.[35] Sadly, this perception did little to mitigate the practical cruelty of medieval warfare and in practice the presumption that if one side was 'just' the other side must be 'unjust' and undeserving of mercy was commonly made even if it was not logically inherent in the doctrine.[36]

With all these weaknesses, there was nonetheless a clear sense of the possibility of culpable wrongdoing in the conduct of warfare – war crimes as they would now be termed. A number of instances can be advanced in support of this proposition. An early example may be seen in the Penitential Decrees issued by the Western church after the battles of Soissons (923) and Hastings (1066).[37] There even developed a *jus armorum* which had some functional similarity to the modern *jus in bello*, although it was rather more concerned with notions of 'chivalry' than with practical humanitarianism.[38] In the late medieval era the remarkable *Hagenbach case* in 1415, in many ways the first 'international' war crimes trial, stands out.[39] The proceedings included both archaic and strikingly

---

[34] St Thomas Aquinas, *Summa Theologica*, 2a2ae.40,1., in A.P. d'Entreves (ed.), *Aquinas: Selected Political Writings*, trans. J.G. Dawson, (Blackwell, 1959), 81.

[35] See above, note 32.

[36] See above.

[37] For detailed discussion see G.I.A.D. Draper, 'Penitential Discipline and the Public Wars of the Middle Ages', (1961) April / May *International Review of the Red Cross*.

[38] See P. Contamine, trans. M. Jones, *op. cit.*, n. 7, at 284–92.

[39] For discussion see G. Schwarzenberger, *International Law, Vol. II, Armed Conflict*, (Stevens, 1968) at 462–6.

modern elements, ranging from a discussion of the obligations arising from an oath of knighthood to a discussion of a 'defence' of superior orders which would have been by no means out of place at Nuremberg or Tokyo, or, indeed, before the International Criminal Tribunals for former Yugoslavia and Rwanda in the 1990s.

Ultimately medieval Christian 'just war' doctrine presents a mixed image of good intentions and a practice which was in many cases at best dubious. Finally it failed in its objective both as a result of abuse and because of the violent institutional changes of the sixteenth century which cut the basic bedrock of assumption from beneath it and led to the savage interdenominational conflict of the Thirty Years War. Out of this trauma there emerged the early modern, post-Westphalian, international legal order which was essentially secular in tone, although it was by no means necessarily a complete break from what had gone before.

IV. Just War Doctrine and the Transition to the Early Modern Era

The sixteenth century marked in many ways a time of transition in European development. The intellectual ferment of the Renaissance was followed by the ecclesiastical and political division of Europe along radically new lines in the course of the Reformation. It is by no means a coincidence that this was accompanied by a strongly renewed emphasis upon national identity, even if this was more a change of perception than of political reality. In the following century the accumulated political and confessional tensions exploded in the Thirty Years War which had a contemporary European impact at least equivalent to that of the First World War in the early years of the twentieth century. That great disaster ended with the 1648 Peace of Westphalia which is conventionally, if artificially, taken to mark the formal commencement of the early modern era in international law. [40]

The failure of constraints upon resort to armed force was an important issue in sixteenth- and seventeenth-century juristic thought. The ultimate reshaping of the international (European) legal order is conventionally associated especially with the work of Hugo Grotius (1583–1645), but this is a considerable oversimplification. [41] Grotius built upon the work of earlier theorists, including in particular the writings of members of the sixteenth-century Spanish School such as Francisco

[40]   For discussion see L. Gross, 'The Peace of Westphalia 1648–1948', (1948) 42 *American Journal of International Law*, 20.

[41]   For analysis of the significance of Grotius' work see H. Bull, B. Kingsbury and A. Roberts (eds.), *Hugo Grotius and International Relations*, (Oxford University Press, 1990).

de Vitoria[42] and Balthazar Ayala,[43] as well as the writings of Alberico Gentili,[44] an Italian protestant working in Elizabethan Oxford. Grotius, however, wrote at a time which was, of necessity, prepared for radical change, and he has therefore gained the exaggerated title of 'father of international law' when he was, rather, one of a number of significant thinkers who moulded a climate of opinion from which the distinctive early modern era in the development of public international law emerged.

Grotius himself recognised three just causes of war: defence in case of actual or imminent injury to the State; recovery of lawful entitlements of the State and the punishment of States in delict. There was nothing new in this and even his contention that a subject might be duty-bound not actively to participate in an unjust war is paralleled, e.g., in the work of Belli, who was himself relying upon earlier authority.[45] Despite this, it cannot be doubted that Grotius had, in practice, an important impact upon the conceptualisation of the new international legal order of the seventeenth century and, in the present context, his closeness to earlier bellum justum thinking is thus a matter of importance. The nature of the change in thinking about war which occurred in seventeenth-century Europe merits emphasis. The collapse of the late medieval European order in the turmoil of the Renaissance and the Reformation generated a significantly altered jurisprudence and, specifically, revised ideas of the forms of obligation imposed by law.[46]

The extent of the development of early modern *jus ad bellum* doctrine can be seen in the mid-eighteenth-century work of Emer de Vattel (1714–67). In *Le Droit des Gens, ou Princips de la Loi Naturelle, appliqués à la Conduite et aux Affaires des Nations et des Souverains* published in 1758[47] he affirmed the strict limitations supposedly imposed upon the right of States to wage war. He stated that,

[42] His principal work in this area was *De Indis et de Jure Belli Reflectiones*, published posthumously in 1565, published in a modern edition, (ed., E. Nys) trans. J. Pawley Bate, in The Classics of International Law series (Carnegie Institute of Washington, 1917).

[43] His major work was *De Jure et Officiis Bellicis et Disciplina Militarii*, published in 1582, published in a modern edition, trans. J. Pawley Bate, in The Classics of International Law series (Carnegie Institute of Washington, 1912).

[44] See *De Jure Belli*, published in its final form in 1598, published in a modern edition, trans. F.W. Kelsey *et al.*, (Oxford, 1933).

[45] P. Belli, *De Re Militari et Bello Tractatus*, Part II, ch. II, citing Baldus, *On Feuds*, Book I, Title V, ch. 1.

[46] For discussion see H. McCoubrey, *The Obligation to Obey in Legal Theory*, (Dartmouth, 1997), ch. 3.

[47] Published in a modern edition, ed., J.B. Scott, trans. C.G. Fenwick., in The Classics of International Law series (Carnegie Institute of Washington, 1916).

> If men were always reasonable they would settle their quarrels by an appeal to reason; justice and equity would be their rule of decision, their judge. The method of settling disputes by force is a sad and unfortunate expedient to be used against those who despise justice and refuse to listen to reason . . . A wise and just Nation, a good ruler, will only use it as a last resort . . .[48]

The ideas of restraint upon resort to armed force, and moderation in its use, advanced but by no means uniformly practised during the eight-eenth-century European 'Enlightenment', collapsed at the turn of the eighteenth and nineteenth centuries with the French revolutionary and Napoleonic wars. These wars were upon so large a scale and, at least initially, so much coloured by ideological difference that the earlier customary humanitarianism was excluded. This ushered in the era of which Jean Pictet remarks that,

> . . . there would be mass wars, with vast collisions between entire peoples who had assembled all their material and emotional resources to destroy one another. . . . Thus began the epoch of wars of 'unbridled ferocity' as Marshal Foch[49] described them. This period was marked by a terrible setback for humanitarian principles.[50]

This is in some ways an oversimplification, in that many of the post-Napoleonic wars of the nineteenth century were neither very large in scale nor particularly ideological in their origins. The callousness of the nine-teenth century was the product in reality of the combination of an incompetence and institutional brutality displayed with appalling clarity in the 1854–5 Crimean war. The despatches of Russell from the Crimea to *The Times* of London revealed much of this. So too did the private correspondence of many who were at the battle front and were appalled by what they saw. Amongst them was the British military surgeon Edward Mason Wrench, whose letters to his family paint a horrifying picture of the quality of the military medical services at the time.[51] In the second half of the century modern international humanitarian law affording some protection for the victims of armed conflict began to take shape, in particular, but not only, through the work of Henry Dunant following the battle of Solferino in 1859. The American Civil War also led to major developments in the mitigation of armed conflict, including the highly praised Lieber Code,[52] which served as an early model for significant later

---

[48]   *Ibid.*, Vol. III, 243.

[49]   One of the French senior commanders in the First World War.

[50]   J. Pictet, *Development and Principles of International Humanitarian Law*, (Martinus Nijhoff, 1985), 24

[51]   See H. McCoubrey, 'Before "Geneva" Law: A British Surgeon in the Crimean War', (1995) 304 *International Review of the Red Cross*, 69–80.

[52]   US Army General Order 100 of 1863. For discussion see G. Best, *Humanity in Warfare*, (Methuen, 1963; first published by Weidenfeld & Nicolson, 1980), especially at 155–6, 170–1, 247–8, 258–9.

jus in bello development. In the present context, however, the American civil war requires to be treated with some caution. The conventional misapprehension that this was a 'just war' fought to liberate the slaves in the southern states can be a source of distortion in discussion of the ethics of the conflict. The question of liberation was in fact a late development in a conflict essentially fought over the balance of power between federal and state governments and the claims to godliness made during the conflict had, perhaps, more to do with American culture than theology *stricto sensu*. Be that as it may, in the context of international relations the legalistic post-Westphalian *jus in bello*, failed to limit the incidence of war and, like its scholastic predecessor, tended increasingly to serve more as an excuse for than a constraint upon aggression. The brutal climax to this course of development occurred at the beginning of the twentieth century with the horror of the First World War. Thereafter the structure of the *jus ad bellum* changed dramatically, first with the false dawn of the era of the League of Nations, which included most importantly the renunciation of war as a legitimate instrument of policy with the 1928 Pact of Paris, and, following the renewed trauma of the Second World War, the establishment of the United Nations.

V. A Christian View of the Modern *Jus ad Bellum*

From the trauma of the two World Wars there emerged the modern *jus ad bellum* or, more accurately, the *jus contra bellum*. The Covenant of the League of Nations after 1918 did not, strictly, outlaw resort to armed force although it discouraged it strongly. The Preamble to the Covenant indeed placed first amongst the objectives of the States forming the League the achievement of 'international peace and security by the acceptance of obligations not to resort to war . . .' Article 12(1) of the League Covenant was somewhat equivocal in requiring submission of any dispute 'likely to lead to a rupture' to arbitration or judicial settlement with no resort to war until three months after such a decision should have been rendered. It may also be noted that the League Covenant made provision, by Article 16, for a system of collective security similar in principle to that set up, through much more detailed provision, by Chapter VII of the United Nations Charter.[53] Unfortunately, perhaps, the League system of collective security rapidly lapsed into desuetude in the face of the aggressive totalitarian powers of the 1930s, more through a failure of political will than through any inherent weakness in the provision. On the rare occasions on which the League did take firm action it achieved a degree of success[54] which suggests that

[53] See below.

[54] The resolution of the Graeco-Italian Corfu crisis in 1923, following the murder of General Tellini and policing of the Saarland Plebiscite in 1935,

the fatalism which paralysed the organisation in its later days was neither inevitable nor wholly justifiable. A formal ban upon resort to armed force as a mode of international dispute resolution came only with the 1928 Pact of Paris[55] which was closely reflected in the Charter of the International Military Tribunal at Nuremberg in 1945 which, by Article 6(a) included within its jurisdiction,

> Crimes against Peace: namely, planning, preparation, initiation or waging a war of aggression, or a war in violation of international treaties, agreements or assurances, or participation in a common plan or conspiracy for the accomplishment of [war crimes or crimes against humanity] . . .

In dealing with military aggression under Article 6(a) the Tribunal relied upon the 1928 Pact of Paris as a statement of established international law,[56] and the principle has never been openly doubted since that time.

After the Second World War the United Nations Charter repeated the ban upon resort to armed force in international relations by Article 2(3)(4). These paragraphs of Article 2 provide that,

> (3) All Members [of the United Nations] shall settle their international disputes by peaceful means in such a manner that international peace and security, and justice, are not endangered.
> (4) All Members [of the United Nations] shall refrain in their international relations from the threat or use of force against the territorial integrity or political independence of any State, or in any other manner incompatible with the Purposes of the United Nations.

This means that armed force is precluded as a legitimate mode of dispute resolution and, very emphatically, forbidden as aggression against another State. The provision made for the maintenance of international peace and security by Chapter VII of the UN Charter, specifically by Articles 39–42, represents an advanced form of collective security, building upon the earlier and unsuccessful structures of the League of Nations. Article 39 provides that the UN Security Council is to determine where there is a threat to or breach of the peace and decide what action, under Articles 41 or 42, should be taken in response to it. A determination under Article 39 supposes that a negotiated settlement under Article 33 has either failed or been overtaken by events. Measures in response to a threat to or breach of the peace under Article 41 are peaceful in nature and would, typically, involve economic sanctions. It may, however, be noted that these are not necessarily to be seen as a more humane or 'loving' option, as the

---

54   *(continued)*   which probably averted an early outbreak of war between France and Germany, may be cited as examples. See G. Scott, *The Rise and Fall of the League of Nations*, (Hutchinson, 1973), 85–8 and 296–301.

55   Also known as the Kellogg-Briand Pact.

56   Judgment of the International Military Tribunal (1946), 1 IMT. 219–20.

effects of post-1991 sanctions against Iraq may be thought to demon -
strate.[57] Where such measures either have proved inadequate or manifestly
would do so, the use of military force to restore or maintain international
peace and security can be authorised under Article 42. In practice this
staged progression of response has never quite functioned as the proce -
dure is set out in the UN Charter. The ideological blockages of the
post-1945 'cold war' effectively impeded Security Council action in
many ways, especially when it came to the authorisation of force under
Article 42. In addition to this, the provision of forces by Member States,
in effect, on standby for UN action under Article 43, was never
implemented to the extent or in the way apparently intended. The end
result has been that the use of force for peacekeeping or peace-making
has generally involved *ad hoc* forces with significant problems of internal
organisation[58] and has been authorised with careful vagueness 'under
Chapter VII' of the Charter without stating under quite which provision
thereof. An example of this may be seen in the establishment of the
NATO-led Implementation Force (IFOR) in former Yugoslavia in place
of the UN Protection Force (UNPROFOR) by UN Security Council
Resolution 1031 of 15 December 1995. The Resolution states very
simply that the Security Council was 'acting under Chapter VII of the
United Nations'. However these Chapter VII provisions may have been
modified and even damaged by the effects of the former 'cold war', the
present practice still represents a system of collective security against
aggression, and the use of force by or with the consent of the UN in this
context may be seen as a form of international policing action. [59]

In the context of immediate responses to acts of aggression by States,
rather different questions arise in the interpretation of Article 51 of the
UN Charter which are in some ways more troublesome from a Christian
perspective. Article 51 provides that,

> Nothing in the present Charter shall impair the inherent right of individual
> or collective self-defence if an armed attack occurs against a Member of the
> United Nations, until the Security Council has taken measures necessary to
> maintain international peace and security.

'Measures' thus taken are to be reported immediately to the UN Security
Council and do not in any way 'affect the authority and responsibility'
of the Council. The defects and ambiguities of the drafting of Article 51

---

[57]   See N.D. White, 'Collective Sanctions: An Alternative to Military
       Coercion', (1994), XII International Relations, 75–91
[58]   See H. McCoubrey and N.D. White, *The Blue Helmets: Legal Regulation of
       United Nations Military Operations*, (Dartmouth, 1996), chs. 6 and 7.
[59]   For extended discussion of this issue see N.D. White, *The United Nations and
       Maintenance of International Peace and Security* , (Manchester University Press,
       1990).

are too large a subject for full discussion in the present context.[60] Two questions are, however, of immediate relevance. One is the question of when for this purpose an armed attack 'occurs'? Is it, for example, permissible to launch an attack to ward off anticipated aggression whilst still remaining within the remit of 'self-defence'? The right of self-defence preserved by Article 51 is stated to be 'inherent' and therefore *ex hypothesi* predated the UN Charter. At the same time it must clearly also be subject to the pacific norm enshrined in the 1928 Pact of Paris and Article 2(4) of the Charter itself. The danger of doctrines of anticipatory self-defence lies in the possibility that at some point anticipatory responses to perceived threats become themselves acts of aggression and if Article 51 is taken to authorise such action it defeats a central purpose of the Charter of which it is part.

Legal doctrine upon this matter derives from *The Caroline incident*.[61] The *Caroline* was a US ship which was being used by private parties to ferry men and equipment into Canada with a view to instigating insurrection there. A British force crossed into US territory, set the *Caroline* on fire and pushed it over the Niagara Falls. The United States protested and Britain replied that the action had been a legitimate exercise in self-defence. After negotiations the two governments were agreed that self-defence was a response to an instant, overwhelming necessity leaving no time for deliberation or choice of means. They continued to disagree as to whether the action against the *Caroline* satisfied this criterion, but Britain made a formal apology for the infringement of US territorial sovereignty and the matter was dropped. There is no reason to think that Article 51 in any way expands the *Caroline* concept of self-defence but this still leaves open the meaning of overwhelming necessity. In the *Nicaragua case*[62] the International Court of Justice reserved the question of anticipatory self-defence, but the majority of the Court clearly favoured a more restrictive rather than a broader view. The broader view has been advanced in defence of a number of unilateral uses of force, including the attack by Israel upon Iraqi nuclear power plants under construction in 1981 and the US invasion of Grenada in 1983. These arguments must, however, be considered at best dubious and an extension of what the wording of Article 51 appears in its context to intend. Even granted that, there remains the question of when an armed attack 'occurs' for this purpose. In the context of modern military technologies, if a State were required to wait until missiles were actually landing and exploding in its territory the time for effective defence might well have passed before

---

[60]   For discussion see D.W. Greig, 'Self-Defence and the Security Council: What does Article 51 Require?' (1991), *40 International and Comparative Law Quarterly*, 366–402.

[61]   Moore, *Digest of International Law*, Vol. II, at 412.

[62]   [1986] ICJ Reps. 3.

action was permitted. The only useful answer that can be given to this is that defensive action will become permissible at the point when armed attack is clearly imminent, even if it has not actually at that point been perpetrated. This is, of course, no more than a restatement of the *Caroline* principle but it is, perhaps, the best which international law offers at the present time. It means of course that sending troops and other military resources to an ally in anticipation of a threat is not an exercise of the right of self-defence under Article 51 – that will arise only when military action is undertaken. Thus, the build-up of coalition resources in Saudi Arabia in the context of the Iraqi invasion and occupation of Kuwait in 1990 was not as such a matter pertaining to Article 51, or indeed to any other provision of Chapter VII of the UN Charter. When force was used to eject Iraqi forces from Kuwait it was done under Security Council Resolution 678 of 29 November 1990, which provided by paragraph 2 that the Security Council 'acting under Chapter VII of the Charter'.

> AUTHORIZES Member States cooperating with the Government of Kuwait, unless Iraq on or before 15 January 1991 fully implements . . . the foregoing resolution [demanding its withdrawal from Kuwait], to use all necessary means to uphold and implement resolution 660 (1990) and all subsequent relevant resolutions and to restore international peace and security in the area.

The careful phrasing may again be noted, especially with regard to Chapter VII of the Charter, but it is clear that the coalition acted within a Security Council mandate, which is a 'measure' superseding the operation of Article 51, which had been the original basis for coalition preparations pursuant to a request for assistance from the Emir of Kuwait.

Is this structure of collective security compatible with Christian doctrine, or does the combination of the love command and our Lord's rebuke to Peter in the garden of Gethsemane delegitimise it? It is the contention of the present writer that the relevant provisions of the UN Charter are in fact compatible with Christian teaching as it is to be applied in the existing condition of international relations. In the first place, military aggression is unequivocally forbidden in a manner which is in effect a simple expression of love of neighbour. Where, however, aggression in fact occurs, love of enemies does not mean acquiescence in or implicit collaboration with their wrongdoing – such a response would ultimately be loving neither to the erring 'neighbours' nor, certainly, to their victims. At the same time it must be asked whether the scope of legitimate response ends at prevention and reversal of the effects of the aggression or whether it extends, in some sense, to the infliction of punishment. It is proper at this point in the argument to ask what is meant by 'punishment' in this context. If military action in itself is intended as a punitive act, in some sense a very large-scale act of reprisal, it is clearly forbidden by both Christian teaching and public international law. Vengeful retributiveness cannot be an expression of love or of forgiveness. Under customary international law, represented by the *Naulilaa* case[63] a punitive 'reprisal' was rendered unlawful if the means adopted were disproportionate and excessive. Under the UN Charter there is no room for punitive raids of this nature. [64] Punishment of individuals for their criminal acts, as by the International Military Tribunal at Nuremberg and the International Military Tribunal (Far East) at Tokyo in 1945 or by the International Criminal Tribunals for former Yugoslavia and Rwanda in the 1990s are another matter, but these do not involve the collective punishment of a country by acts of war.

Military action against an aggressor may, in the present condition of international relations, be accepted as *necessary* if always regrettable in the course of a Christian analysis. At the level of interaction between individual human beings one may, and should, pray for the repentance and regeneration of a murderer or a rapist, but at the same time it is hardly inappropriate to stop their acts of murder or rape. The point may be illustrated with an extension of the parable of the good Samaritan. What if the good Samaritan had arrived not some time after the mugging on the Jericho road, but whilst it was going on? The obvious interna-tional comparison is with the Munich Agreement of 30 September 1938. The British and French Prime Ministers, Chamberlain and Daladier, betrayed a small democratic ally into the clutches of the Third Reich and rendered it impossible for it to resist. From the viewpoint of former Czechoslovakia, however, whether this was so or not there was a large appearance of 'peace at any price' – so long as that, extortionate, price was to be paid by someone else. This was not even a case of the Samaritan following the example of the priest and the Levite and ignoring the wounded victim, it was rather a case of holding the victim down so that the mugging might proceed more efficiently. Who was the neighbour of Czechoslovakia in 1938? Most certainly not Britain or France.

It can be urged that prayer is indeed the only response to military aggression and, as said above, it is indeed a proper Christian response. If, however, nothing else is expected it seems a curious view of prayer, a theological 'Jim'll Fix It' enjoining quietism in the face of evil. One would expect that the Christian parents of a seriously ill child would pray for him or her, one would also expect them to seek medical assistance without being accused of denying thereby the power of prayer. There was much prayer in and for Nazi-occupied Europe between 1939 and 1945. Those prayers were answered when the Nazi regime was over-thrown by the Allied armies – even granted the many doubtful moral qualities of the Allies themselves.

---

[63]   (1920) 2 UNRIAA, 1013.
[64]   See *The Corfu Channel case* (1949), ICJ Reps., 4, especially at 35.

In summary, the analysis of the *jus ad bellum*, or, more accurately, the *jus contra bellum*, here advanced is that Christian teaching absolutely forbids military aggression, as does modern public international law. Where, however, the unlawful and sinful act of military aggression has in fact been perpetrated, assistance and defence of the victim, including the population for which a government is responsible may, in the present state of the world, be not only permissible but even a duty. Wars of aggression can never for a Christian be anything other than a violation of divine command, but passivity in the face of attack or manifest gross threat may be not only a callous disregard for friends and others for whom responsibility is taken but also ultimately a lack of love, or concern, even for the wrongdoers themselves. This does not mean that enemies, including in particular individual enemy soldiers, sailors and air force personnel, are therefore inherently to be considered 'evil' or even any more sinful than we ourselves. They and we are both sinners and the victims of sin. This perception must, necessarily, inform a Christian view of the *jus in bello*, the law governing and seeking to limit the conduct of armed conflict. The question then remains of how love of enemies is to be expressed where hostilities have in fact broken out.

The answer is in essence fairly obvious. Even in the midst of the Second World War prayers were said in churches for ultimate reconciliation with the enemy, in consciousness of the fact that both sides would finally stand side by side before the judgement and mercy of God. It may be recalled also that, as remarked above, St Augustine counselled that a just cause may be rendered unjust if it is pursued in a cruel and vengeful spirit. The modern *jus in bello*, in its attempts both to constrain and mitigate the methods and means of warfare and its endeavours to protect the victims of armed conflict, can well be seen as an expression precisely of that basic, but all too frequently ignored, Augustinian caveat.

VI. The Viability of a Humanitarian *Jus in Bello*

The modern *jus in bello* comprises 'Geneva' provision for the protection and assistance of victims of armed conflict, meaning the wounded, sick and / or shipwrecked, prisoners of war and civilians; and 'Hague' provision for the limitation of certain methods and means of warfare. The two divisions of the *jus in bello* are closely linked in many respects, e.g., in their provision for the protection of civilians, and in view of their common humanitarian aims they are now referred to collectively as international humanitarian law. This law is, it must be emphasised, very much the secondary office of the modern laws of war. It seeks to impose some measure of humanitarian mitigation where the primary endeavour of aversion of armed conflict has failed. The *jus in bello* is thus in no sense an *alternative* to the *jus ad bellum*. It is a response to the immediate consequences of failure to avert war. Two immediate questions require to be addressed as preliminary issues. Is a humanitarian law of armed conflict possible and, even if it is, might it not serve to facilitate war by making it seem more 'acceptable'?

Some commentators, including many Christians, have been con-temptuous of the humanitarian *jus in bello*, deeming it to be a contra-diction in terms. Writing in the mid-nineteenth century of the experience of the 1812 Napoleonic invasion of Russia, the novelist Leo Tolstoy aptly summarised this view in his comment in *War and Peace* that,

> From the time [Napoleon] . . . took up the correct fencing attitude in Moscow and instead of his opponent's rapier saw a cudgel raised above his head, he did not cease to complain to [Fieldmarshal Prince] Kutuzov and to the Emperor Alexander that the war was being carried on contrary to all the rules, as if there were any rules for killing people.[65]

This is in the end a rather crudely stated reflection of the view commonly, but not entirely correctly, attributed to the strategic theorist Carl von Clausewitz, who, in his classic work *Vom Kriege* (On War), published posthumously in 1832, is taken to have argued that war as an act of violence is inherently incapable of ethical or legal restraint. In fact von Clausewitz wrote that,

> If one side [in war] uses force without compunction, undeterred by the bloodshed it involves, while the other side refrains, the first will gain the upper hand. . . . That is how the matter must be seen. . . . If wars between civilized nations are far less cruel . . . the reason lies in the social conditions of the states and in their relationships to one another. These are the forces that give rise to war; the same forces circumscribe and moderate it. They themselves however are not part of war; they already exist before fighting starts.[66]

The important caveat to Clausewitz's primary statement is frequently missed or ignored. His point is that armed conflict does not occur in a moral, social and political vacuum but within and between human societies which, even in the extreme exigencies of armed conflict, retain certain basic ethical norms. In short, war taken as a phenomenon in isolation may indeed be logically incapable of limitation in its own terms, but in the real context in which it in fact takes place it is subject to a variety of both ethical and pragmatic limitations. The ethical limitations should to some degree be obvious and derive from the fact that human societies do not move from a utopian condition of peace to a limitlessly barbaric condition of war, but rather lapse into violent

[65]   Tolstoy, *War and Peace*, (Moscow, 1868–9) trans. L. and A. Maude, (Macmillan, 1943), Book XIV, ch. 1, 1139.

[66]   C. von Clausewitz, *On War*, ed., and trans., M. Howard and P. Paret, (Princeton, 1976 and 1984) ch. 1, 75–6.

confrontation whilst yet retaining an involvement between human beings. The implications of this complex interaction are considered further below. The pragmatic limitations arise, *inter alia*, from the fact that belligerent States must still engage in international relations and by outrageously cruel conduct, direct or indirect, may suffer loss of support and ultimately even pariah status. The varying, and varyingly appropri-ate, treatment of both Iraq and Serbia–Montenegro [67] in the 1990s may serve as provisional examples of this phenomenon. Such cruelty may actually be counter-productive even in straightforward military terms. The point was put succinctly by the late Klaus Kuhn in his remark that, 'the quickest way of achieving and maintaining a lasting peace is to conduct hostilities humanely . . . It is evident that humanitarian considerations cannot be dissociated from the strategic concept of military leaders.' [68] It may further be added that this same point answers completely the objection sometimes heard that international humani-tarian laws of armed conflict assist the ruthless by impeding the law-abiding. In fact, unmitigated ruthlessness is by no means necessarily efficacious and, in any event, the norms of international humanitarian law do not serve to frustrate the attainment of any legitimate military objective in the course of armed conflict.

The question of whether an international humanitarian law of armed conflict has the deleterious effect of making war seem 'acceptable' is a complex question, to which, it is suggested, a negative answer must ultimately be returned. This idea, in effect that the worse the horrors of war are permitted to be the less likely will be the occurrence of war, may be discounted upon even the most superficial view of the last 100 years of historical experience. If sheer horror were enough to put an end to war it is difficult to imagine that war could have continued beyond, e.g., the Somme campaign in the First World War. It is sadly the case that wars are rarely if ever caused by the people directly involved in fighting them or by those who are 'collateral' victims of hostilities. To argue against humanitarian mitigation upon such a basis is ultimately a cruel utopianism to be comfortably asserted at a great distance from the ugly realities of warfare.

VII. A Christian Appreciation of the *Jus in Bello*

The first point to be made about the modern international humanitarian laws of armed conflict is their impartiality of application. The fact that

---

[67] Serbia–Montenegro still considers itself the Federal Republic of Yugoslavia.
[68] K. Kuhn, 'Responsibility for Military Conduct and Respect for International Humanitarian Law', *Dissemination*, August 1987, (International Committee of the Red Cross), 1.

the only legitimate use of military force is either *defensive* in character or, under the direction of the UN Security Council, under Chapter VII of the UN Charter for the restoration or maintenance of international peace and security is fundamental to the structure of the *jus ad bellum*, but cannot affect the application of humanitarian norms in armed conflict. Such considerations cannot be utilised to invite the twisting of ideas which beset scholastic *bellum justum* theory and ultimately sought to deny humanity and mercy in the treatment of opponents. It is worth noting that in modern secular international law the Preamble to 1977 Protocol I Additional to the 1949 Geneva Conventions states that,

> . . . the Geneva Conventions of 12 August 1949 and of this Protocol must be fully applied in all circumstances to all persons who are protected by those instruments, without any adverse distinction based on the nature or origin of the armed conflict or on the causes espoused by or attributed to the Parties to the conflict.

This is an obvious humanitarian requirement – it is also one clearly concordant with the command of Jesus for love of neighbour as spelt out in the, here very directly applicable, parable of the good Samaritan. Even in the tainted 'just war' tradition some reference is found to such a concept, as, e.g., in the writings of St Augustine of Hippo.[69]

Even in the Old Testament, which often condones destruction of enemies (Deut. 20; Num. 31:7–19; and 1 Sam. 15), there are some signs of compassion towards enemies (2 Kgs. 6:21–23; Exod. 23:4–5; and Prov. 25:21) in keeping with the present provision of the Third Geneva Convention of 1949 making provision for prisoners of war. A detailed analysis and critique of Old Testament teaching and practice on war is beyond the scope of this chapter. Reconciling the Old Testament with the New Testament teaching on the need to love our enemies, referred to above,[70] is also a task for theologians outside the scope and space constraints of this chapter.

The more recent development of humanitarianism in armed conflict has proceeded very unevenly over time.[71] A relative degree of humanitarian principle was achieved in the European dynastic wars of the eighteenth century, not least because these were relatively small-scale and in some sense 'professional' wars devoid of ideological content. The view of King Louis XV of France at the battle of Fontenoy in 1747 that enemy wounded should be treated, 'exactly like our own men, because

[69] See above.

[70] See text accompanying n. 9–13 above. Some light is shed on the difficult Old Testament passages on treatment of enemies in F.D. Kidner, *Hard Sayings: The Challenge of Old Testament Morals*, (IVP, 1972) at 40–45.

[71] For a useful historical review see G. Best, *Humanity in Warfare*, (Methuen, 1983; first published by Weidenfeld & Nicolson, 1980).

when they are wounded they are no longer our enemies.'[72] may be considered one of the positive indicators from the period of the European 'Enlightenment'.

At the turn of the eighteenth and nineteenth centuries, with the large-scale and much more embittered French revolutionary and Na - poleonic wars, such basic humanitarianism did not entirely disappear but was both weakened in concept and much reduced as the minimal relief resources of the day were overwhelmed. A mid-nineteenth-century nadir was reached with the mixture of incompetence and callousness which produced the horrors of the Crimean and Franco-Austrian wars. The upturn came in the 1860s. The work of Florence Nightingale at Scutari during the Crimean war, along with that of the Sisters of St Vincent de Paul with the French army and of the Nursing Order of the Exaltation of the Holy Cross, set up by the Tsar's aunt the Grand Duchess Helena Pavlovna, with the Russian army began to improve the medical services under a significantly Christian inspiration. The great leap forward occurred, however, after the 1859 Franco-Austrian war with the *ad hoc* rescue work organised by Henry Dunant on the battlefield at Solferino, which saved the lives of many *on both sides*. Dunant went on to write a pamphlet, *Un Souvenir de Solferino*, in which he urged (1) an international treaty for the protection of the wounded and sick in armies in the field, and (2) an international organisation to supplement military medical provision for the assistance of the wounded and sick in armed conflict. The result of this was the first, 1864, humanitarian Geneva Convention and the establishment of the organisation which was to become the international Red Cross. This branch of the humanitarian laws of armed conflict, known as 'Geneva' law expanded and is now based in the four 1949 Geneva Conventions and the two 1977 Protocols Additional thereto. The four Conventions make protection respectively for the wounded and sick on land, the wounded, sick and shipwrecked at sea, prisoners of war and civilians. These groups are all characterised by the fact that they either are or have been rendered *hors de combat* and are in this rather strict sense victims of armed conflict. The two 1977 Additional Protocols make supplemen - tary provision to that offered by the 1949 Conventions, dealing respectively with international and non-international armed conflicts.

The provision is too extensive for detailed exposition in this chapter, but an idea of the basic principles may readily be afforded. In relation to the treatment of the wounded and sick on land, Article 12 of 1949 Geneva Convention I provides that,

[The wounded and sick] shall be treated humanely and cared for by the Party to the conflict in whose power they may be, without any adverse distinction

---

[72]   Quoted by J. Pictet, *Development and Principles of International Humanitarian Law*, (Martinus Nijhoff, 1985), 22.

founded on sex, race, nationality, religion, political opinions, or any other similar criteria. Any attempts upon their lives, or violence to their persons, shall be strictly prohibited; in particular, they shall not be murdered or exterminated, subjected to torture or to biological experiments; they shall not wilfully be left without medical assistance and care, nor shall conditions exposing them to contagion or infection be created. Only urgent medical reasons will authorize priority in the order of treatment to be administered.

Virtually identical provision is made for the wounded, sick and ship-wrecked at sea by 1949 Geneva Convention II, Article 12. Article 13 of 1949 Geneva Convention III prescribes the humane treatment of pris-oners of war and forbids their maltreatment, humiliation or subjection to acts of reprisal. No single such citation emerges from 1949 Geneva Convention IV in relation to civilians, partly because of the greater range and complexity of their circumstances, but the same principles are found embedded in a number of distinct provisions. The protection of civilians was significantly expanded by 1977 Protocol I Additional to the 1949 Geneva Conventions and a fundamental principle which can be traced at least back to the Land Warfare Regulations annexed to 1907 Hague Convention IV, if not, indeed, to the 1868 Declaration of St Petersburg, is now stated unequivocally by Article 48 of the Protocol which provides that,

> In order to ensure respect for and protection of the civilian population and civilian objects, the Parties to the conflict shall at all times distinguish between the civilian population and combatants and between civilian objects and military objectives and accordingly shall direct their operations only against military objectives.

Such measures as use of civilian internees, or prisoners of war, as 'human shields' for military installations, as was done in some cases in the 1990–91 Gulf Conflict, are clearly illegal.[73] It is not suggested that present humani-tarian provision is wholly adequate – there are those who argue, for example, that a new Convention or Protocol is needed specifically for the protection of women in armed conflict.[74] Like any area of law, international humanitarian law is in a continuing state of development as, sadly, is the experience of war. The protective provisions of interna-tional humanitarian law are of course vastly more extensive and complex

---

[73]   See 1949 Geneva Convention III, Article 23; 1949 Geneva Convention IV, Article 28; and 1977 Additional Protocol I, article 51(7). For discussion of 'human shield' abuses in the 1990–91 Gulf Conflict see F.J. Hampson, 'Liability for War Crimes', in P. Rowe (ed.), *The Gulf War 1990–91 in International and English Law*, (Routledge with Sweet and Maxwell, 1993), 241–260.

[74]   See J. Gardam, 'Women and the Law of Armed Conflict: Why the Silence?' (1997), 46 *International and Comparative Law Quarterly*, 55.

than so brief an indication might seem to suggest,[75] but space forbids a detailed analysis in the present context.

The principles and provisions of modern international humanitarian law would, it is suggested, immediately be recognised by any good Samaritan as an expression of practical love of neighbour and are as such not only compatible with Christian teaching but actually commanded thereby. It must of course be stated at once that the Geneva Conventions are not as such Christian documents, nor is the Red Cross a Christian organisation. The Conventions and the organisation are wholly impartial in their humanitarian commitment, irrespective, *inter alia*, of creed. Their work is, however, clearly something to which any Christian should warm. In this context it may be added that the cross in the Red Cross is used as an identificatory emblem and is not intended to have any religious significance. The official Red Cross position, as stated by Article 53 of 1949 Geneva Convention I, is that the red cross emblem is a 'tribute paid to Switzerland by the adoption of the reversed Federal colours' but this has all the appearance of an *ex post facto* rationalisation. The actual origins of the emblem are very uncertain. Pierre Boissier suggests that the adoption of the red cross emblem by the 1863 Geneva Conference was made in addition to Dr Appia's proposal of a simple white arm band by General Dufour,[76] but Jean Pictet suggests that the emblem was proposed by the Prussian delegate, Dr Loeffler, during a recess.[77] Whoever suggested it, however, the emblem clearly was not intended as a religious symbol. Despite this most Muslim countries, starting with the Ottoman Empire during the 1876 Turko-Serbian war, have objected to it and use the red crescent as an equally recognised alternative. The authorities in Saudi Arabia during the 1990–1991 Gulf Conflict attempted to compel coalition forces there to remove red crosses from their ambulances and medical facilities, but this was successfully resisted.[78] The former Shah of Iran also objected, and in preference Iran used the red lion and sun emblem, which was also recognised as a protective emblem.[79] This, however, was abandoned after the Iranian revolution and the modern Iranian military medical services use the red crescent emblem. Israel has objected to both the red cross and red crescent emblems and uses instead the red star of David. This is not officially recognised as a protective emblem but was accepted as such *de facto* by the Arab powers during the various Arab-Israeli wars.

[75] For discussion see H. McCoubrey, *International Humanitarian Law*, (2nd ed., Ashgate, due 1998).

[76] P. Boissier, *History of the International Committee of the Red Cross*, Vol. I, *From Solferino to Tsushima*, (Henry Dunant Institute, 1985), 77.

[77] J. Pictet, *Development and Principles of International Humanitarian Law*, (Martinus Nijhoff, 1985), 30.

[78] *The Independent*, (London), 16 December 1990.

[79] See 1949 Geneva Convention I, Article 38.

In parallel, and frequently overlapping, with the 'Geneva' limb of international humanitarian law there is also its 'Hague' division which seeks to impose humanitarian restrictions upon methods and means of warfare – meaning tactical conduct and weapons types and usage. Such law has two principal dimensions. One is to restrain the use of certain weapon types which would inflict (militarily) 'unnecessary' suffering. The other is to ensure that certain basic rules are observed which enable protective signs and emblems to be respected and understood. This fundamental principle of 'unnecessary suffering' which underlies 'Hague' law, and in many ways 'Geneva' law too, is found in the Preamble to an early arms control treaty – the 1868 Declaration of St Petersburg – which bans small-calibre anti-personnel explosive projectiles. It is known as the principle of 'unnecessary suffering'. The Preamble states that,

> [T]he only legitimate object which States should endeavour to accomplish during war is to weaken the military forces of the enemy . . . this object would be exceeded by the employment of arms which uselessly aggravate the sufferings of disabled men, or render their death inevitable . . . the employment of such arms would, therefore, be contrary to the laws of humanity.

This is a cogent statement of the basic nature of the humanitarian *jus in bello*. Its purposes are at once limited and profound. It does not seek a utopian unrealism in reference to an activity which is in its nature a harshly cruel exigency of human relations. It does seek to confine the cruelty of war to its own minimum sphere and even within that to minimise suffering to that level which reasonably cannot be avoided, *granted the existence of that situation*. Apart from the St Petersburg ban upon small calibre explosive projectiles, which inflict a much more tearing and damaging wound than an ordinary rifle bullet, the principle is to be seen directly in, e.g., the ban upon 'dumdum' bullets imposed by 1899 Hague Declaration 3, the ban upon Chemical and Biological warfare now found in the 1925 Geneva Gas Protocol (following the catastrophic failure of 1899 Hague Declaration 2 in the First World War) and reinforced, with new provision also upon manufacture and stockpiling, in the 1972 UN Biological Weapons Convention and the 1992 UN Chemical Weapons Convention. The most recent development in this specific area has been the framing bans and restrictions upon blinding laser weapons and land mines in additional Protocols to the 1982 UN Conventional Weapons Convention. 'Hague Law' also protects certain recognised modes of communication between belligerents, as in the use of the white flag, as well as flags and military insignia of the enemy, under Article 23(f) of the Land Warfare Regulations annexed to 1907 Hague Convention IV.

The protection and relief of victims seems in the context of war to be a basic application of the imperative of love of neighbour. The Samaritan in the parable was a *prima facie* enemy of the Jew who had been mugged on the Jericho road and yet he had pity upon him and gave him help and treatment in his predicament. The comparison with, e.g., the medical treatment of an injured enemy soldier would seem here to be both simple and direct. The same point may be made, through somewhat more complex analogies, for the humane treatment of prisoners of war and vulnerable civilians. Limitation of methods and means of warfare, as a means of mitigating the severity of combat, may also be seen as at least a qualified 'love of enemies', bearing in mind that even in the harsh exigencies of war it is at least conducive to an ultimate reconciliation.

VIII. Conclusions

It has been contended in this chapter that although armed conflict is in itself both an illegal and unchristian state of international relations, just as violent confrontation is an unacceptable form of interpersonal relations, it cannot always in the present condition of the world be avoided. Where, notwithstanding international morality and law, military aggression does take place, a defensive military response may not only be unavoidable but may even be an ethical duty. Certainly the victim of international military aggression should no more be left piously unassisted than should the victim of personal aggression in a mugging in the street. From a Christian point of view, where, tragically, wars do occur, the assistance of the victims and the mitigation of the horrors of war may thus be suggested to be not only acceptable to Christians but a fundamental Christian duty. In this sense the modern *jus ad bellum*, which at least aims towards the achievement of neighbourliness in peace, and the interna-tional humanitarian *jus in bello*, which aims to relieve the victims of warfare, may be seen as no more than complex expressions of the command that we should love our neighbour as ourselves – meaning truly as we ourselves are loved – in a particularly difficult circumstance.

Undoubtedly Christians should work for peace, which is not by any means the same thing as acquiescing quietly in the perpetration of aggression. The true shape of Christian defence policy, and the law deriving from it, may be seen ultimately as one of rendering itself unnecessary. In the same way the ultimate success of a police force would be to terminate crime and render much of their function obsolete. If there were no fear of aggression, there would be no need for defence, but pending such a better state of things the necessity for 'justified response', in contrast with the evil proclivities of 'just war' doctrines, seems inevitable. Whilst that is so, both the *jus ad bellum* and the *jus in bello* as they now exist must seem both necessary and in their substance well worthy of Christian support. It must finally be remembered that all those who may be engaged in armed conflict remain human beings who are in need, possibly very great need, of pastoral care. Soldiers, sailors and air force personnel engaged in defence assume a great burden on behalf of their fellow-citizens. In seeking ultimately to lift that burden from them

Christians should, in both our understanding of doctrine and in our practice of pastoral care, be mindful of those who carry it for us. In the practice of warfare there must also, ultimately, be mindfulness of the enemy. In a sinful order an active response to evil may be necessary. Indeed the love command of our Lord is an active not a passive norm, and resistance is by no means necessarily incompatible with love. In 1940 prayers were said in English churches for reconciliation with the enemy and for an end to the evil which had first overcome them when Nazism took over the German Reich, remembering that both the allies and the axis in the Second World War would one day stand before God and hear his judgement. Against that standard all international relations and law must be set. The very existence of laws of armed conflict is a telling symptom of the fallen character of the present order of international relations. Within that order they may be seen as both needful and beneficial, even as we wait and pray for a new order in which those necessities shall have ceased.

Subject Index

Biblical Index

Christian Perspectives on Law Reform
Edited by Paul R. Beaumont

In his foreword Lord Mackay of Clashfern, a former reforming Lord Chancellor, argues that much can be learned by considering our laws in the light of biblical perspectives.

The various contributors in this volume set out to demonstrate this principle in a wide range of topical issues which include the compatibility of evangelicalism and social concern; the question of whether a Bill of Rights should be introduced in the UK; recent moves in favour of euthanasia in the USA and Australia; environmental law and corporate governance.

This book will enable people to analyse contemporary legal issues from a Christian perspective rooted in biblical principles.

"This book is an important contribution to a neglected perspective on law and law reform . . . a diverse series of scholarly and thought-provoking analyses of contemporary issues which challenges many widely-held assumptions and offers new insights for law reform."
Ian Leigh, Professor of Law, Durham University

Contributors are Teresa Sutton, Senior Lecturer in Law at the University of Westminster; Julian Rivers, Lecturer in Law at Bristol University; Professor John Warwick Montgomery, Professor Emeritus of Law and Humanities at the University of Luton; David Harte, Senior Lecturer in Law at the University of Newcastle; Stephen Copp, Senior Lecturer in Law at Bournemouth University.

Paul R. Beaumont is Professor of European Union and Private International Law at the University of Aberdeen and the Scottish Co-ordinator of the Lawyers' Christian Fellowship. He is co-author of *Private International Law* and *EC Law* among other works.

ISBN 0-85364-852-2

paternoster press